THE
BOOK
THAT
CONQUERED
TIME

How the Bible Came to Be

ROB SUGGS

WHITAKER
HOUSE

THE BOOK THAT CONQUERED TIME
How the Bible Came to Be

www.robsuggs.com
robsuggs@gmail.com

ISBN: 979-8-88769-043-8
eBook ISBN: 979-8-88769-044-5
Printed in the United States of America
© 2023 by Rob Suggs

Whitaker House
1030 Hunt Valley Circle
New Kensington, PA 15068
www.whitakerhouse.com

Library of Congress Cataloging-in-Publication Data
Names: Suggs, Rob, author.
Title: The book that conquered time : how the Bible came to be / Rob Suggs.

Description: New Kensington, PA : Whitaker House, [2023] | Includes
  bibliographical references. | Summary: "Traces the Bible's history from
  ancient parchments to modern translations, examining differences and
  similarities between the Jewish holy books and the Christian Bible, how
  the New Testament writings were copied and collected, including the
  apocryphal gospels and letters, and church controversies and disputes
  over the ages"— Provided by publisher.
Identifiers: LCCN 2023017493 (print) | LCCN 2023017494 (ebook) | ISBN
  9798887690438 | ISBN 9798887690445 (ebook)
Subjects: LCSH: Bible—History. | BISAC: RELIGION / History | LITERARY
  CRITICISM / Subjects & Themes / Religion
Classification: LCC BS445 .S84 2023 (print) | LCC BS445 (ebook) | DDC
  220.9—dc23/eng/20230606
LC record available at https://lccn.loc.gov/2023017493
LC ebook record available at https://lccn.loc.gov/2023017494

1 2 3 4 5 6 7 8 9 10 ⊔⊔ 30 29 28 27 26 25 24 23

DEDICATION

This book is lovingly dedicated to the people of
Second-Ponce de Leon Baptist Church,
and its rich history of pastors, teachers, and everyday saints,
who taught me to love the Word of God.

CONTENTS

1. An Abiding Word 7

2. In the Beginning Were the Words 15

3. A National Library 24

4. The Prophets Fall Silent 36

5. Letters of Hope and Promise 50

6. Four Portraits, One Savior 62

7. Faith of the Fathers 78

8. A Battle of Ideas 92

9. The Library Is Closed 104

10. The Word Set Free 117

11. In Plain English 131

12. The Bible, in Other Words 147

Bibliography 163

Appendix A: Selective Timeline of Biblical History 166

Appendix B: The Amazing Story of Codex Sinaiticus 170

About the Author 176

1

AN ABIDING WORD

Howard Rutledge's feet touched the earth, his body followed, and his parachute deflated softly behind him. And from every direction, the villagers came running, shouting, their farming tools in hand. Howard knew this was no welcoming party.

It was 1965, and Howard was a Navy pilot. His Vought F-8 Crusader had been shot down one hundred miles south of Hanoi. The crowd fell upon him, beating him with sticks and fists, stripping away all of his clothing, and finally dragging him, bruised and bleeding, toward a cage.

This was the beginning of seven years of imprisonment, mostly in the notorious "Hanoi Hilton." He was given little more than thin soup to eat. Rats and spiders were everywhere. He shivered through frigid winters and coiled his inner strength the best he could when the soldiers came for him, for it always meant another round of physical abuse and interrogation.

Other servicemen occupied adjoining cells, and when no guards were around, there were whispered conversations. But Howard's hopes for survival were fading. Maybe his time had come. He found himself clinging to the idea of the next world, the heavenly afterlife he'd learned about in church, back in Oklahoma. It was all he had now. Howard began to scour his memory for hymns and Bible verses, and he wished he knew more. "Amazing Grace," John 3:16, "O Come All Ye Faithful"—these things had never seemed so important before now.

Soon he was sharing his verses and hymns with his nearest neighbor, Harry Jenkins, who was also collecting them. Each gem scooped up from the recesses of memory was a lost jewel recovered.

One day, Harry issued a low whistle. It was a signal meaning *news*. As soon as the guard was away, Harry told Howard, "I've remembered another one: Ruth and Naomi!"

"Fantastic! Tell me."

And Harry began to share what he could remember of the story of these two women from long ago who found themselves alone in a land that wasn't their own, yet found comfort and the real presence of God. Howard felt a surge of warmth and hope. He and Harry weren't unlike Ruth and Naomi—two women in the Bible who leaned upon one another in frightening times and found strength in God. Later, in his memoir *In the Presence of My Enemies*, he wrote that he lived off that one story for days.

And the story was spread up and down the cells, so that it could be added to everyone's collection. That was the wonderful part; what one remembered, all could share. Some of the others had added verses, songs, a simple biblical idea. Nearly everybody knew Psalm 23 and the Lord's Prayer, but anything extra was a true blessing.

Together, these men assembled a bare-bones, rudimentary Bible that provided strength and a spiritual shield that no guard could snatch away.

Thus, in war-torn Southeast Asia, a handful of North American soldiers shared ancient writings from Israel. And nothing about that seemed odd or unusual. After all, across the world, hundreds of millions of people were doing the same thing, though with a bit less urgency.

These people attended church weekly to hear preaching based on those words. And during the week, they spoke in streams of phrases and figures of speech that originated in this Book—phrases such as *the writing is on the wall; scapegoat; apple of my eye; eat, drink, and be merry; Good Samaritan; my cross to bear; reap what you sow; the root of the matter; skin and bones;* and untold others. As the prisoners of war whispered between cells, they likely used all kinds of biblical phrases and ideas without even realizing it.

We all do. Certain phrases of the Scriptures are deeply embedded in the English language. The King James Version came along at a key moment in the evolution of the language. The British spoke what is now known as Early Modern English. It was the dialect of Shakespeare, of brilliant poets such as Milton and Donne. The translators of the KJV wanted, among other things, a Bible that delighted the ear and took firm hold in the memory. They succeeded.

This was also the age of musical and artistic giants, who inevitably chose biblical stories and topics for their paintings and oratorios. It was a time of exploration, when the Bible traveled on ships to distant ports.

Literacy was on the rise, and people were eager to read the Bible for themselves. The heartwarming, life-altering words of these pages dissolved directly into the English language until they began to guide the formation of our sentences and reasoning. And the words we choose, in turn, guide our thinking, reasoning, and decision-making. *Faithful in small things, given larger things* is a biblical concept. Sacrificial love is an idea from the Scriptures. Our idea of *the human condition*, also known as sinfulness, originates in the Bible. We think of linear time, of one life with heaven beyond, because the Scriptures present that view of the universe.

Just take a look at the numbers from an international research data and analytics group:

+ 100 million Bibles are printed annually.
+ There are 140 percent more Bibles in print today than there were in 1975.
+ Thirty-eight Bibles are sold every minute.
+ Nearly 55,000 Bibles are sold daily.
+ 115,000 Bibles are given away daily.
+ There are more than 80,000 versions of the Bible in the world that sell at least one unit annually.[1]

1. "32 Bible Sales Statistics," WordsRated, February 2, 2022, wordsrated.com/bible-sales-statistics.

We can no more deny the place of this Book in our culture than we can argue away the floor beneath our feet. Both are foundations on which daily life is built. Thus a great many people who would never think to pick up a Bible, or walk into a church, have been molded by the words of Scripture far more than they realize. They may deny God, but they still conceive of a world set forth by the Bible. It's all they've ever known.

THE INESCAPABLE WORD

After so many centuries, the Bible is still faithfully studied. Most homes contain one; some have several. Genealogies are found in family Bibles that have been handed down for generations. Missions and societies specialize in making the Book available everywhere possible. Since 1908, for example, Gideons International has distributed more than two billion Bibles to inns, motels, and other venues.

As a result of all this, billions of copies of the Book fill the shelves and bedsides of the world. Yet the Bible continues to be a top seller, year after year. As a matter of fact, an American bestseller typically sells several thousand copies in a week. The Christian Bible, on the other hand, sells nearly twenty *million* copies per year—many times the pace of a bestseller. From one year to the next, it outsells every other publication, without exception.

And what's the Book about? The first part of the Bible, in particular, covers the history of a relatively small nation in the Mediterranean world, from its beginning to its occupation by Roman troops, as well as its poetry, its guidance for life, and its prophecy.

The second part of the Book describes the life of one teacher from that nation, His life and teachings, and the beginning of the movement He founded. Most of today's readers of the Book consider themselves members of that movement and followers of its Teacher.

And where are the original manuscripts of these writings? They're dust in the winds of time. None exist. Yet the writings traveled to this time and place across thousands of years, copied and translated, and shared by each generation, casting off the various languages bearing them like wrapping paper from an old and precious gift. Today, the Book that conquered time is translated into nearly three thousand languages. It's read and shared in ways that would have astonished its writers, through computers, on social media, and in audiobooks. One particular Bible app is found on more than five hundred million computer devices across the world.[2]

Yet if all those copies of the Bible, all the apps, and all its various forms were somehow to vanish simultaneously in the next moment, its imprint would remain on every part of life. The Western calendar measures time before and after the year then thought to mark the birth of Jesus (*anno Domini*, "year of the Lord"); the civil calendar is adapted from the Gregorian calendar, created within Catholicism.

But there are other biblical fingerprints, so common we'd almost fail to notice them. The idea of the value of the individual, on which Western thought is founded, is derived from the first pages of the Bible, as is the concept of one God who isn't so much occupied with fertility and sacrifice as with love, grace, and service. He stands out from other ancient deities in that way, and it can be said that modern values are shaped in His image. It's found in the Book, which we've had all along.

Our conception of humanity is also just as the Bible describes it. We are created in God's image and capable of goodness, yet prone to the chronic acts of rebellion we know as sin.

So many biblical ideas are simply ingredients in the cultural air we breathe. We take them for granted without crediting them to their source in the Scriptures. The concept of public education began in medieval communities, where the church provided education as well as early hospitals. Biblical ideas of justice, compassion, and charity lie at the root of Western democracy.

---

2. Jerry Pattengale, "Gutenberg, meet Gruenewald. App builder's YouVersion puts Bible in half-billion phones," Religion News Service, November 19, 2021, religionnews. com/2021/11/19/gutenberg-meet-gruenewald-app-builders-youversion-puts-bible-in-half-billion-phones.

The Magna Carta of 1215, which establishes the freedom and worth of the individual, is rooted in the Bible. Thomas Paine's *Common Sense*, often cited as the inspiration for the American and French revolutions, is powerfully influenced by the biblical idea that all people are created equal. That understanding isn't typically found in societies apart from those inspired by scriptural concepts.

Social reforms such as the abolition of slavery were inspired by men and women carrying biblical convictions. There's no overreach in stating that the Bible has shaped the modern world more than any other influence, yet it is so dominant that its points of impact are nearly invisible.

THE TIMELESS WORD

This Book of books has held its own through thousands of years of civilization, providing an eternal fire that never burns out. Over all the centuries—from oral tradition to paper to digital information—that flame has illuminated whatever medium and language carried it. Whenever those fall away, the flame simply moves on to the next means of ministry.

Thus the ancient and timeless Word of God has moved along through an unending procession of languages and presentations, outlasting them all. Kingdoms and empires have risen and fallen while that flame continued to glow, as bright and attractive as ever, drawing people to the light of life. Against all seeming odds, the rise of science has done nothing to eclipse this timeless volume and the beliefs it lays out. The introduction of other religions and philosophies has never come close to threatening the popularity of its teaching.

Yet when we thumb through the Book, we find it's something of a hodgepodge, a diverse library running to nearly eight hundred thousand words. Though written over many centuries, the works reflect the long-gone culture of a Western Asian pocket of land roughly equivalent to the acreage of Vermont.

The earth has contained many thousands of such communities since the dawn of civilization. But this one, among them all, is still of central importance to us. We know the names of Israel's kings, prophets, and heroes. We're acquainted with now-obscure tribes such as the Philistines and religious groups such as the Pharisees and Sadducees. We know the dimensions of Solomon's Temple and understand the life of a first-century fisherman. And we understand the special reasons why tax collectors were despised.

We know all of these details not because they're important in themselves, but because they help us understand the greater story: God's relationship with a nation over thousands of years. We understand that the life story of this one nation encompasses the life story of this entire world. After all, the Book begins with the creation of the universe and closes with the end of time itself. Ultimately we embrace this long-ago time and culture because it speaks to our current-day time and culture.

We need to know what a *talent* was worth and the size of a mustard seed so that we can better understand the urgent truth Jesus was getting at in His parables. It's also important for us to know how God related to King David, his virtues, and his sins because we're certain that God relates to us in much the same way.

The Bible says of itself, "*The grass withers, the flower fades, but the word of our God stands forever*" (Isaiah 40:8). This is yet another prophecy that has proven to be true. Isaiah's words don't constitute a command. They don't tell us that the Word *should* be protected or preserved forever, though it has been both. It says the Word "*stands forever*"—active voice rather than passive. The Word carries the power and authority of heaven. It's a living thing, enduring through the rise and fall of any particular nation or movement.

The Word stands when its admonitions embolden the first generation of Christians to hold true to their faith even in the face of martyrdom.

It stands when a German monk, in the year 1517, reads it, insists on honoring its truth, and begins a world-shaking reformation of the Christian church.

It stands when it bolsters the faith of American soldiers in a Vietnamese concentration camp.

It stands when young couples gather around to study in someone's home, and a struggling marriage finds strength and hope.

It stands when its words take root in a child's heart, through a story told in Sunday school, and guides that child throughout her life, so that even as the world grows darker and more complex, God's light shines through that child.

It stands because God ordains it, because its words carry His power, and its precepts never fail. To live out the teachings of this Book is to find peace, contentment, and blessing in all things. For that reason, we want to know more about the Bible. We're curious about its life and times, its journey from etchings on a stone to writings on papyrus to the unfolding of parchment scrolls to the pages we read today.

Humanity has changed a lot during all that time. How is it that this Word remains unchanged, fully powerful, fully wise?

The unforgettable story is worth the telling.

2

IN THE BEGINNING WERE
THE WORDS

The Bible speaks of a place where God crowned His created world with human life. Genesis 2:8 says that in the wilderness of the world, He planted a garden and placed His children there.

A general location for that garden is suggested in Genesis 2:11–14: the source of a river that flows out into four branches. The first two we cannot trace; the latter two are known to us: the Tigris and the Euphrates. This suggests that the first place where humanity knew its Father was in the region of Mesopotamia.

Science and archaeology tell a similar story. This region of Mesopotamia is known as a *cradle of civilization*, for here, the hallmarks of civilization first showed themselves. Farming, with all of its methods and approaches, began to develop. People began to gather in centers where labor could be divided, large buildings could be built, and distinctive art could be created—the first cities. And finally, words found their way into the craft of writing. These three developments are generally considered the marks of a civilization coming of age,[3] and we find their oldest traces in the Fertile Crescent of ancient Mesopotamia.

These developments established a new and compelling identity for the human race. They said, in essence, "This is humanity, with its questing mind, its curiosity, its growing understanding of its environment. These are people, not to be confused in any way with the animal kingdom. These are men and women who reflect a sophisticated

3. "Key Components of Civilization," *National Geographic*, accessed May 16, 2023, education.nationalgeographic.org/resource/key-components-civilization.

creation. They are joining together, creating society for mutual pro-tection and exchange of ideas, and they are constantly learning."

These were also people who looked within themselves and into the skies, and were capable of profound questions and deep reflec-tions, such as the following words addressed to God:

> *What is man that You are mindful of him...? For You have made him a little lower than the angels, and You have crowned him with glory and honor. You have made him to have dominion over the works of Your hands; You have put all things under his feet, all sheep and oxen—even the beasts of the field, the birds of the air, and the fish of the sea that pass through the paths of the seas.*   (Psalm 8:4–8)

Such self-understanding and evaluation is the mark of intelli-gence. The poet sees his superiority to all the creatures of the earth, and even his responsibility for them. He is, even so, "*a little lower than the angels.*" In other words, he finds himself in a precarious place between heaven and earth—a creature, a creation, but a special one. He knows the dust of the earth, and he also knows the existence of spirit.

All things considered, he wonders what is in him that God, who is above all things, would be "*mindful of him.*" After all, this same poet, King David, can write these words:

> *Wash me thoroughly from my iniquity, and cleanse me from my sin. For I acknowledge my transgressions, and my sin is always before me. Against You, You only, have I sinned, and done this evil in your sight...Behold, I was brought forth in iniquity, and in sin my mother conceived me.*   (Psalm 51:2–5)

These are the words of a man who feels the reality of guilt. He feels the filthiness of sin, and he longs to feel clean again. He under-stands that only God can restore this cleanness. Yet he also realizes that sin is an indelible presence in his life, something born with him.

Both these statements come from a writer—a king, no less—who lived one thousand years before Christ. He shows a comprehension of human character that is not unique but is actually shared by all his people and reflected in the full library of that nation's writings that have come down to us. Upon virtually every page are these themes of sin and purity, humanity and its loving, reaching God.

Humanity, we're told, is created in the image of that God. We are crowned *"with glory and honor"* (Psalm 8:5) and given dominion over all earthly creation. Men and women are made to enjoy a special relationship with their Father in heaven. Yet simultaneously, this same humanity is tragically flawed, born in sin and given to disobedience. Along with God's grace and forgiveness, the very pattern of it defines all these writings.

This description of human character hits the mark for many people. Three thousand years later, we understand, like King David, what it means to be capable of both loving devotion and hateful evil. We understand his longing for a better, purer life because we share it.

Who were the writers of these deeply perceptive words? They were these same Semitic-speaking people who came from the Mediterranean area of civilization. We first discover them living in the land of the Canaanites, beside the Mediterranean Sea. And they're the very people credited with the greatest leaps from Bronze Age primitivism to civilization, through their farming, their building of population centers—and most of all, their remarkable, unforgettable writing.

FROM SPEECH TO SYMBOLS

The written word stands as one of the most revolutionary of human inventions. Voltaire called it "the painting of the voice."

Creating a graphic system for transmitting ideas meant records could be kept, messages could be sent, and histories could be preserved. And in the great scheme of things, the revelation of godly wisdom could be passed down more surely from one generation to another.

It's writing, above all things, that creates the reality of civilization and propels humanity on its march toward a progressive future. One generation can leave behind its thoughts and experiences for its successors to build upon.

At some point, some man or woman received the inspiration to lift a finger and trace, perhaps in the sand, a symbol that signified a meaning. It was probably in the form of a representational image. This small beginning opened the door to a vast universe of possibilities. And because people wrote and recorded, we know things about them that would otherwise be lost to history.

We can imagine families and villages, before the age of the written word, gathering around campfires at night, telling stories, and sharing the experiences of their lives. Stories passed down from one generation to another are called "oral traditions," and we still enjoy them today. We hear little anecdotes about our grandparents, or even great-grandparents, and we share them with our children. Yet how many details do any of us really know from the lives of our direct ancestors three or four generations back? No matter how charming or significant their stories may have been, they've tended to last no more than a generation or two.

But with the development of the written word, it became possible to safeguard the legacy of our stories and our wisdom—and a *higher* wisdom.

For the ancient Hebrew people, a small segment of the Mediterranean population, writing carried a particular significance. It was a divine imperative.

Then the LORD *said to Moses, "Write this for a memorial in the book."*   (Exodus 17:14)

Then the LORD *said to Moses, "Write these words."*
                                                            (Exodus 34:27)

And you shall write very plainly on the stones all the words of
this law.   (Deuteronomy 27:8)

Throughout the Scriptures, we find a God who insists on record-keeping. We are told that He *"is Spirit"* (John 4:24), and that for Him, *"a thousand years are like a day"* (2 Peter 3:8 NIV). Human generations pass in procession before Him, none possessing the memories of their forebears. God knew we needed a way to connect with the hard-won wisdom of our past. While we must learn the great lessons of living for ourselves, we still need more than simple everyday experience.

We need revelation.

We need to know what God is like, and we need to understand how He interacts with us across time. We need to know what's non-negotiable rather than subject to interpretation, opinion, or prefer-ence—commandments like loving our parents, worshiping God, and not lying, stealing, or committing adultery. These were and are truths worth writing down.

God appointed and raised a nation, and He gave it a mandate to list these nonnegotiable commands so that even as people pass from this earth, His law would never do so.

The grass withers, the flower fades, but the word of our God
stands forever.   (Isaiah 40:8)

STONE, FIBER, SKINS, AND HEARTS

The development of writing passed through a number of stages. The first known system of writing was *cuneiform*, which featured symbols impressed on clay tablets. Most of what we know about early civilization comes from cuneiform tablets that have been recovered, and the information that can be translated from them. The Black Obelisk of Shalmaneser III shows Jehu, an Israelite king, and allows us to place actual dates on passages in the Bible.

The earliest finds show systems using symbols and images rather than actual letters and alphabets. These are called *pictographs* or pictograms. Simple visually recognizable designs might represent cattle or crops, and these were used primarily for recordkeeping. Egyptian pictographs are called hieroglyphs.

But this was still a step away from what we think of as writing. Inevitably, the limitations of these symbols would have become evident, and more sophisticated ideas were used. Alphabetic scripts began to appear during the second millennium BC.[4] People could express thoughts and ideas of great complexity through the spoken word; at some point, they began to seek methods for doing the same in more permanent media.

The earliest forms of writing yet found have been recovered in biblical (Semitic) lands. The oldest known sentence written in the earliest alphabet reads as follows: "May this tusk root out the lice of the hair and the beard." These words are inscribed on a fine ivory comb no more than an inch and a half long that was found in 2016 in South-Central Israel.[5]

The modern English alphabet has twenty-six letters, but ancient alphabets were created to evoke as many as thirty phonetic sounds. Different cultures had their own alphabets, though when trading across broad regions began to develop, it became necessary to standardize these. Phoenician merchants, who traveled constantly, adapted the system used in biblical lands and helped make it the most common alphabet. The Greek and Aramaic alphabets developed from this.

It was the Greeks who first introduced vowel sounds into alphabets. In earlier times, only the "hard" sounds of consonants were deemed necessary for writing, not the vowels that represented the "soft" sounds we make between them. When we read the ancient

4. Jan van der Crabben, "Alphabet," *World History Encyclopedia*, April 28, 2011, www.worldhistory.org/alphabet.

5. Katie Hunt, "Bronze Age comb reveals an ancient frustration with head lice," CNN, November 8, 2022, www.cnn.com/2022/11/08/world/lice-comb-discovery-earliest-sentence-alphabet-scn/index.html.

words of biblical Hebrew, therefore, we find nothing but consonants. Adding vowel sounds made languages far more versatile and flexible.

The earliest human pictographs and images are written on stone. Religious laws and civil laws, intended for permanency, were often etched into rock, and some of these have been located. A calendar has been found in the area of Palestine, memorializing the seasonal activities of farmers in what seems to be a form of poetry. There's also King Hezekiah's S-shaped tunnel that once piped water into the city of Jerusalem. (See 2 Kings 20:20; 2 Chronicles 32:30.) An inscription celebrating this accomplishment was made around 700 BC.

Twice during the days of Moses and Joshua, God instructed those two leaders to place large stone memorials, cover them in plaster, and write God's law upon them. (See Deuteronomy 27:2–3; Joshua 8:32.) And sure enough, history tells us that ink on plaster-covered stone had a period of popularity for writing.[6]

But clay was more popular still. It was more readily available, of course; it was soft for writing and could be baked to hardness. There are biblical references to clay tablets as well. For purposes less formal than religious laws—say, a contractual agreement between two herdsmen—clay tablets would be ideal. Still, however, there were limitations. The tablets were breakable, and how much could be written upon them was limited.

Wood and metal, even silver and gold, were other options. Two small silver amulets in the shape of scrolls have survived. One includes the blessing found in Numbers 6:24–25: "*The* Lord *bless you and keep you; the* Lord *make His face shine upon you, and be gracious to you.*" This discovery comes from the late Old Testament period (about 500 BC) and constitutes the oldest biblical inscription.

PAPYRUS AND PARCHMENT

Almost any hard surface could be written upon, really, but how could someone write at length?

6. "Egyptian materials and pigments," Royal Society of Chemistry, accessed May 16, 2023, edu.rsc.org/resources/egyptian-materials-and-pigments/1621.article.

That's where *papyrus* came in. This plant-based material came from reeds growing most prominently around the Nile River in Egypt. The famous story of baby Moses being placed in a basket to float in the river among the reeds may be referring to the very plants used to make the first light, flexible, yet fairly durable writing material. (See Exodus 2:3.) Black carbon ink was made by mixing soot, water, and plant or tree gum. The Egyptians valued papyrus for more than writing; it was a national symbol and often used to decorate architecture.

Papyrus was laid out in strips, pressed together, smoothed into a paper-like substance, and then dried. The idea for making this material caught on across Mediterranean culture. In all probability, most of the New Testament was written on papyrus because the Greeks and Romans favored it. Our word *paper* comes from the word *papyrus*, while *Bible*, meaning "the books," came from a Greek term that referred to rolls of papyrus.

Once pages were made, they were laid out and glued end to end to make a roll—a length of papyrus about ten inches high and thirty-five feet long, rolled up in a scroll. With papyrus, longer works such as our biblical books could be created. Matthew's gospel would constitute a full scroll, while a number of Paul's letters would be found together in another scroll. The standard length of a scroll probably influenced the length of books, just as book sizes conform to standards today.

Parchment came next, by way of leather (velum) and other animal skins. Different preparation methods are used to make parchment instead of leather. Chemicals are used to tan leather, but parchment is placed on a frame to stretch and dry it. For valuable documents, parchment provided a smooth page that didn't tear easily. One only needed access to the skins of sheep, goats, or cattle. But it wasn't until a few centuries later that parchment won out as the primary writing material. By then, papyrus had become scarce—today, it no longer grows along the Nile, though it can be found in a few other areas.

The coming of parchment writing also brought on the *codex*, which contained loose sheets that were secured together by various means. This would ultimately replace the scroll and point the way toward the book that we know and love.

It's not possible to overstate the importance of the book to the progress of civilization. Before this, the Romans used wax tablets that were something like modern notebooks made of wood and folded in the middle. A stylus was used for writing on the wax surface and wiping it clean—thus making a *clean slate*. Records and temporary notes could be kept in codices, but pages could be added, and now the codex was basically a book.

In the New Testament era, the four gospels could be contained in one codex. Ultimately, one book, as opposed to a codex, could contain a full Bible. People began using papyrus pages for the codex, but parchment took over in time. Some scholars believe Christians either developed or popularized the use of the codex—another contribution to Western civilization.

There was and is one other medium for preserving the writing of important things: the human heart. God commanded His people to write down His law, preserve the story of His people, and save this information on mediums of every kind. (See, for example, Deuteronomy 17:18; Isaiah 30:8; Habakkuk 2:2; Revelation 1:11.) God wanted to ensure that we would perpetuate His story and ours, so that we would know the facts, the incidents, and the truths. But He also commanded the law to be written on our hearts:

Your word have I hidden in my heart, that I might not sin against
You.   (Psalm 119:11)

In this way, we have a physical version of the Scriptures for the world and an internalized version for ourselves. God commands that His Word be in writing and in hearts and minds.

3

A NATIONAL LIBRARY

The written word made it possible to record and preserve God's Word, so that it could be shared from generation to generation. And as we've seen, the earliest known writings seem to have come from the very place where the Bible's events are recorded as taking place—the general area occupied by ancient Israel and Judah.

The writers of the Old Testament were people eager to take up stylus, pen, and ink to write down what they heard God saying. Not everyone could read; in general, literacy was quite low in the ancient world. But neither were reading and writing uncommon in a society so given to the written word. Recent studies have suggested that as the Hebrew world grew, it enjoyed a higher level of literacy than once thought.

Of course, there was more to write than religious materials. Archaeological finds confirm that the Israelites regularly kept records of genealogies, tax collections, contracts, and the like on papyrus or clay. Sometimes leaders such as Moses or Paul did their own writing; at other times, scribes were used.

Jeremiah was a prophet who used a secretary and scribe named Baruch, who faithfully recorded the prophet's words and also a great deal of historical detail that has helped us know more about Jeremiah's precise time and the issues his nation faced. Interestingly, two clay pieces have been discovered from his time, carrying Baruch's name, seal, and even his fingerprint. These could have been used by the biblical scribe, though there is no way to definitively make that link.

By Baruch's era—toward the time of the Babylonian captivity and the end of the Old Testament period—there was a great deal of writing going on in Israel and Judah. The Jewish people not only recorded and recited their history, whose preservation was now threatened, but they also kept genealogies and civil records of all kinds, which they stored in the temple. Rabbinical conversations and debates were carefully written and stored and can be read to this day.

Even casual Bible readers notice the lengthy family trees that are so common throughout the Book. So many generations were known because they'd been written down. First Chronicles begins with nine full chapters of names and legacies. While these pages may not make for lively reading today, they are important because they show us the connection of generations, and how God's people kept careful and accurate accounts of everyone and everything.

History was serious business because it affirmed the faithfulness of God over time. And because God cared about every individual, every individual had a name and a history worth recording.

A RIVER RUNS THROUGH IT

It's worth looking at these Scriptures from a high vantage point, in brief summary, to learn just what kind of books these are. Through all the history, poetry, and prophecy of the great Book, we can't miss the firm conviction of all the writers that God has a special relationship with the nation of Israel. As a matter of fact, this is the ongoing theme that rushes like a mighty river through the many books that make up our Old Testament. Characters and events are like tributaries that feed into those waters. This is a vast saga, but it's also the world's greatest love story, the suitor being the Lord God, and the object of pursuit being His children.

After the first eleven chapters of Genesis, relating the early history of mankind, Genesis 12 introduces the great, controlling idea: that of a holy covenant.

Now the LORD had said to Abram: "Get out of your country, from your family and from your father's house, to a land that I will show you. I will make you a great nation; I will bless you and make your name great; and you shall be a blessing. I will bless those who bless you, and I will curse him who curses you; and in you all the families of the earth shall be blessed."

(Genesis 12:1–3)

This is no small promise made to one man. It reaches to *"all the families of the earth"* and stretches across time to guarantee a blessing for all people. It can be seen as laying out the agenda for all of the remaining pages of Scripture, including those in the New Testament. Abram's people—who are yet to come at this point—will have special covenant with God. They will be defined by His promise and His guidance toward becoming a worldwide blessing.

There are other covenants: an earlier one with Noah, after the flood; and others with Moses, David, and Jeremiah. But the latter are all renewals of the Abrahamic covenant at key moments in the history of Israel that make the contract more explicit. David is told his descendent will sit upon the throne as part of this blessing. Jeremiah is promised a new covenant, one written on people's hearts; He will be their God, and they will be His people. As time goes on, God shows more of His plan.

A covenant is a binding agreement. The contract between God and His people is a covenant of love, not unlike a marriage. It promises blessing, protection, and a future legacy.

THE RISE AND FALL OF A NATION

It's easy to forget that Abram, who first received this promise, had no context for this message from heaven. We know nothing about his spiritual beliefs before this moment, but we can be certain there was no written revelation from God—no laws, no Hebrew faith at all. Abraham was just a man of his time, a herdsman and a farmer.

He must have known almost nothing about this God who spoke to him, commanded him, and promised him astounding things.

This was all new and required Abram to gather his family and travel to a new home, based on faith. This, too, would have been a perilous task, but he was obedient. From there, his adventures began, and still, a great deal of faith was required—particularly when no children were forthcoming to the aging couple. Where would this nation come from?

As we follow the story, the child does come—Isaac—and from there, we follow the story through the first generations of the covenant family. The Old Testament offers a pattern of highs and lows as these families multiply and become a sizable group. We learn about the ways of God by following the trials and tribulations of families whose very humanity is so recognizable to us.

When Joseph, the last of the founding fathers of the Hebrew nation, is taken to Egypt as a slave, it is in bondage, ironically enough, that the nation explodes in growth. As Exodus, the second book of the Bible, begins, God raises up a prophet named Moses to lead His people to freedom. God has a permanent home for His people.

At this point, at the beginning of a wayward and painful journey to that land of promise, the relationship between God and His nation moves to a new level. He delivers His law to Moses at Mount Sinai, summarized in the Ten Commandments. Now the people can know a bit more about this mysterious God, who up until now has spoken selectively and rarely. He is one God, and none other is to be worshiped. He establishes a Sabbath rest, and He cares deeply about our human relationships, not just the divine one.

He also has a home for His people to call their own. But they must take it, against discouraging odds. Again, there is a test of faith, and after a generation marked by a failure of courage, the Israelites do claim their home—the land we now know as Israel. While they continue to occupy and defend this *promised land*, they ultimately become a monarchy under kings such as David and Solomon. But due to a lack of faithfulness from the people and their leaders, the nation weakens and splits in two. Israel to the north and Judah to the south are weaker as separate nations, and prophets—God's spokesmen—begin to foretell future disaster.

The disaster comes in the form of invasions from Assyria and Babylon. Judah's greatest city, Jerusalem, is sacked, and the temple, its crowning accomplishment, is laid waste. People are hauled into foreign slavery. Toward the end of this saga, the people are allowed to return home. But much rebuilding remains to be done. Yet God is there all along, offering comfort and promising a renewed covenant that will be the fulfillment of all hope, through a man who will bring deliverance, a messiah.

These many pages tell a rather straightforward narrative, if rather dramatic and sweeping. God builds a nation from one man. The nation is much like its greatest king—blessed, gifted, intelligent, and special to God, yet prone to sin and failure. It rises to greatness, and it falls to despair. It looks to the future with hope. David is *"a man after [God's] own heart"* (1 Samuel 13:14), and Israel is that nation, although both have a way of breaking God's heart.

As consistent and whole as the story is, it's not told by a single, well-organized writer with a theme in mind. We receive it through the combination of many writers through many smaller books. Each book, from Genesis to Malachi, is like another pane in a stained-glass window. One must step back to see the full, brilliant picture that is illuminated by heavenly light. We have books of history, poetry, music, profound philosophy, and simple everyday advice, stories of suffering and romantic love. In the foreground or background, the story of God and His people plays out.

And who are these authors? They, too, are many, and they write their pieces across whole centuries. This is, therefore, a diverse and varied library that covers many times, places, and writers, yet one that seems to have a firm direction and consistent message. Simply put, these themes are: God loves His children; He is faithful, but His children are fickle and faithless. Through time, God never gives up on them, and He promises that one day, the great chasm separating heaven and earth will be closed by an ultimate deliverer, someone who will restore the divine relationship once and for all.

SECTIONS IN THE LIBRARY

Exactly what is in this library of books that we know as the Old Testament? The Hebrew faith, Protestant Christians, Catholics, and Orthodox Christians have slightly different lists, but all are traditionally divided into three sections: the Law, the Prophets, and the Writings—known together as the Hebrew Bible or the Christian Old Testament.

+ **The Law** (*Torah*) is the foundation of the library and never varies. It contains Genesis, Exodus, Leviticus, Numbers, and Deuteronomy, and relates the story of creation, the entrance of sin into the world, the great flood, and the coming of the covenant in the story of Abraham and the patriarchs, the founding fathers of Judaism. Then it covers the story of Moses and his leadership in the wilderness, as the Israelites attempt to enter the promised land. Finally, these books contain the law as given to Moses and in greater detail.

+ **The Prophets** (*Nevi'im*) contain the teachings of the spiritual leaders of the Old Testament and the spokesmen for God's will and guidance. The Hebrew Bible lists Joshua, Judges, Samuel, and Kings as the *Former Prophets*, and Isaiah, Jeremiah, and Ezekiel, as the *Latter* or *Major Prophets*. Finally there are twelve *Minor Prophets*: Hosea, Joel, Amos, Obadiah, Jonah, Micah, Nahum, Habakkuk, Zephaniah, Haggai, Zechariah, and Malachi.

+ **The Writings** (*Ketuvim*), or the Wisdom Literature in the Christian tradition, make up the most varied selection of books. There are great differences between the Hebrew and Christian classifications of books that are considered to be in this category. Ruth, Chronicles, Ezra-Nehemiah, Esther, Job, Psalms, Proverbs,

Ecclesiastes, the Song of Songs, Daniel, and Lamentations are all placed in the Hebrew grouping.

In some cases, the use of scrolls influenced these divisions. The twelve Minor Prophets could comfortably fit on one scroll, so they were ultimately considered one book, as we will see. Ezra and Nehemiah, separate books in the Christian world, also made up one scroll and came to be considered one book. The Hebrew Bible considered 1 and 2 Kings and 1 and 2 Chronicles to each be one book.

By the time the early Christians began to agree on which Scriptures to include in their Bible, scrolls were being cast aside for that new invention, the book, and Christian scholars began to make certain changes based on what they felt was appropriate. The book of Ruth was placed just after Judges because the Scriptures established Ruth's story as occurring during that era. The books of Chronicles and Kings were divided in two and placed together.

These changes gave the front section of the Old Testament a historical feel. As a result, Christians often refer to the *books of history*, from Genesis through Esther. The Writings are more specifically known as the Wisdom books, and include only Job, Psalms, Proverbs, Ecclesiastes, and Song of Solomon (or Songs). Daniel, in the Christian tradition, becomes a prophet rather than a *writing*.

There are several books not included in the Christian canon but found in the Catholic and Orthodox churches. Catholics have these historical books: Tobit, Judith, and 1 and 2 Maccabees. They've included Wisdom and Sirach as wisdom books. And among the prophets we find Baruch. These are known as deuterocanonical books, meaning "belonging to the second canon." These books generally fall in that three-century period between our two Testaments, mostly from 200 BC to AD 70, the year the temple was destroyed by the Romans.

With all of these differences and subdivided books, we emerge with the following numbers: thirty-nine books in the Protestant Old Testament; forty-six in the Catholic one; and forty-nine in the Orthodox one.

Hebrew Bible (tanakh)	Protestant Bible	Catholic Bible
Books of Moses (torah)	**Law (Pentateuch)**	**Law (Pentateuch)**
✦ Genesis	✦ Genesis	✦ Genesis
✦ Exodus	✦ Exodus	✦ Exodus
✦ Leviticus	✦ Leviticus	✦ Leviticus
✦ Numbers	✦ Numbers	✦ Numbers
✦ Deuteronomy	✦ Deuteronomy	✦ Deuteronomy
Prophets (nevi'im)	**Historical Books**	**Historical Books**
Former	✦ Joshua	✦ Joshua
✦ Joshua	✦ Judges	✦ Judges
✦ Judges	✦ Ruth	✦ Ruth
✦ Samuel	✦ 1 and 2 Samuel	✦ 1 and 2 Samuel
✦ Kings	✦ 1 and 2 Kings	✦ 1 and 2 Chronicles
Latter	✦ 1 and 2 Chronicles	✦ 1 and 2 Kings
✦ Isaiah	✦ Ezra	✦ Ezra
✦ Jeremiah	✦ Nehemiah	✦ Nehemiah
✦ Ezekiel	✦ Esther	✦ Tobit
✦ The Twelve (Hosea,		✦ Judith
Joel, Amos, Obadiah,		✦ Esther
Jonah, Micah, Nahum,		✦ 1 and 2 Maccabees
Habbakkuk, Zephaniah,		
Haggai, Zechariah,		
Malachi)		
Writings (khetuvim)	**Wisdom Books**	**Wisdom Books**
✦ Psalms	✦ Job	✦ Job
✦ Proverbs	✦ Psalms	✦ Psalms
✦ Job	✦ Proverbs	✦ Proverbs
✦ Song of Solomon	✦ Ecclesiastes	✦ Ecclesiastes
✦ Ruth	✦ Song of Solomon	✦ Song of Songs
✦ Lamentations		✦ Wisdom of Solomon
✦ Ecclesiastes		✦ Sirach
✦ Esther	**Prophets**	**Prophets**
✦ Daniel	✦ Isaiah	✦ Isaiah
✦ Ezra-Nehemiah	✦ Jeremiah	✦ Jeremiah
✦ Chronicles	✦ Lamentations	✦ Lamentation
	✦ Ezekiel	✦ Baruch
	✦ Daniel	✦ Ezekiel
	✦ The Twelve (Hosea,	✦ Daniel
	Joel, Amos, Obadiah,	✦ The Twelve (Hosea, Joel,
	Jonah, Micah, Nahum,	Amos, Obadiah, Jonah,
	Habbakkuk, Zephaniah,	Micah, Nahum, Habbakkuk,
	Haggai, Zechariah,	Zephaniah, Haggai,
	Malachi)	Zechariah, Malachi)

Yet the Hebrew Bible contains only twenty-four books, given the combination of the twelve minor prophets into one, and the combinations of Ezra with Nehemiah and the unified books of Kings and Chronicles.

To stand back and behold this ancient library is to realize the unparalleled literary tradition of the Hebrew people. We have their history, their songs of worship, their lamentations of grief, their poetry, and their timeless storytelling. The biographical accounts of Joseph, Moses, and David, for example, will be read and admired as long as people continue to turn to their Bibles to hear God's Word.

AN OLD TESTAMENT CANON

Our Old Testament, which is the Hebrew Bible, obviously doesn't include every manuscript created in ancient Jewish culture. The group of books we have is a careful selection that has held up well over the centuries. But who selected these books, and when? How did the twenty-four Hebrew texts become canon—the official, selected group?

It's impossible to find a simple answer to that question. For a time, it was suggested that a Jewish council at Jamnia, late in the first century AD, made the final determination about the books that were ultimately included as inspired writings from God, to be used in worship and study. A prominent rabbi, Yohanan ben Zakkai, moved to the city of Jamnia, perhaps just before the temple was destroyed in AD 70.

This was a time of turmoil and dispersion for the Jewish people. Many conventions of ordinary worship, festivals, Scripture reading, and ritual purity were under threat. And there was a certain inconsistency regarding which writings were appropriate for synagogue reading. Everyone read the five books of the Law, but what about the Song of Solomon, for instance, which concerned itself with romantic passion and failed to mention God? What was to be done with the book of Ecclesiastes, expressing a seemingly cynical view about the meaning of life?

For many years, scholars believed there was a Council of Jamnia that answered many questions, including which books made up a Hebrew canon and how to handle synagogue worshipers who believed Jesus was the Messiah. (They were to be cast out.) But in recent years, the Jamnia theory has been discredited. There simply isn't any evidence such a meeting took place.

More likely, the canon became official much as the New Testament eventually would—by proving itself out among its users. In time, there was general agreement about the twenty-four books that eventually (by about AD 70) made up the Hebrew Scriptures. One of the first Jewish writers to acknowledge a canon was the historian Josephus. Among other important works, he wrote a defense of Judaism called *Against Apion* in 95 BC. He mentioned the three divisions of his Scriptures—five books of the Law, thirteen of the Prophets, and four of "hymns." And he defined what neatly fits the definition of a canon:

> For we [the Jews] have not an innumerable multitude of books among us, disagreeing from and contradicting one another, [as the Greeks have,] but only twenty-two books, which contain the records of all the past times; which are justly believed to be divine; and of them five belong to Moses, which contain his laws and the traditions of the origin of mankind till his death...For during so many ages as have already passed, no one has been so bold as either to add anything to them, to take anything from them, or to make any change in them; but it is become natural to all Jews immediately, and from their very birth, to esteem these books to contain divine doctrines, and to persist in them, and, if occasion be willingly to die for them.[7]

7. Flavius Josephus, *Against Apion*, trans. William Whiston (A.M. Auburn and Buffalo: John E. Beardsley, 1895), from the Perseus Digital Library, Tufts University, www.perseus.tufts.edu/hopper/ text?doc=Perseus%3Atext%3A1999.01.0216%3Abook%3D1%3Asection%3D38.

It should be noted that Josephus counts twenty-two books because he combines Ruth with Judges and Jeremiah with Lamentations, as was often done. Otherwise, he describes a selection of books to which none can be added or subtracted. He also qualifies that these books hold "divine doctrines" worth dying for.

When the early Christians spoke of reading Scripture, it was these Hebrew books they had in mind. Josephus was writing during the period when the four gospels were beginning to circulate, and the Christian church was starting to flourish. The writings of Paul, the apostles, and others had authority for the early church, but they were part of contemporary literature and only in the earliest stages of being seen as the Word of God.

The early Christians read the stories of Abraham, Moses, David, and the prophets, and they saw God's wisdom in them. They realized that some prophecies explained Jesus of Nazareth in His messianic role. The New Testament today is sprinkled with Old Testament references because this was the Scripture that the first Christians used as their guide.

Thus, Judaism and Christianity canonized the original Hebrew Scriptures at virtually the same time. And to this day, both religions actively use the Old Testament as inspired, God-breathed Scripture. The books themselves recognize their own divine origin. The writers make it clear in many passages that the Word of God is being written, and that these were books designed to endure:

> *This word came to Jeremiah from the* LORD, *saying: "Take a scroll of a book and write on it all the words that I have spoken to you."*   (Jeremiah 36:1–2)

If they hadn't been considered to be of divine origin, these writings would never have been saved. Yet across time, scribes copied and preserved them, meticulously guarding their accuracy, so that wherever these books were later found, they never varied.

Thus it wasn't surprising when a first-century copy of Isaiah was found in a Qumran cave in 1947. This was one of the greatest archaeological finds in history—a full, preserved manuscript at least two thousand years old. And in all essentials, it matched the book of Isaiah as found in modern Bibles. It cannot be argued that it's impossible to know what was truly written in the ancient world; the Isaiah scroll, untouched all this time, proves that we can trust the Bible in our hands.

Yet out of the Hebrew texts, a new body of Scripture began to form. It carried the fulfillment of all that was promised to Abraham and his descendants. But that time was still four centuries away as the Old Testament era concluded with the book of the prophet Malachi around 420 BC. Catholic and Orthodox readers of books such as 1 and 2 Maccabees can discover what was happening during this period, known as the intertestamental era; the Protestant Bible is silent.

The land of God's people was anything but quiet. This was a period of incredible turbulence, in which there were no more prophets, many more enemies, and a Jewish rebellion against a Syrian king and a Greek dynasty.

4

THE PROPHETS FALL SILENT

The last book of the Old Testament bears the name of Malachi. This means *my messenger,* so Malachi may have been the name of a prophet or simply the description of one. Either way, this closing book presents a bleak picture of desperate times.

The temple priests have grown corrupt. The people have turned away from the law given to Moses and become apathetic. After all, look around: the once-great nation of David and Solomon has become a spiritual wasteland, a land bullied by other empires and their gods.

But the book of Malachi includes a promise from God:

> Behold, I will send my messenger, and he shall prepare the way before me: and the LORD, whom ye seek, shall suddenly come to his temple, even the messenger of the covenant.
>
> (Malachi 3:1 KJV)

Thus, the final messenger of the Old Testament foretells the first messenger of the New Testament: John the Baptist. And somehow, *"the LORD…shall suddenly come to his temple."* Malachi didn't explain how; that's not the work of prophets but of time.

With these final chapters of the long Old Testament saga, silence falls, at least as far as the Protestant Bible is concerned. There were still books written during this period, and they make valuable reading. From the Jewish perspective, however, the prophets themselves were mum.

As we turn the page, we find ourselves in the Gospels.

That doesn't mean the times in Palestine have been uneventful. They were actually filled with transition and turmoil, so as we begin to read the stories of Jesus, we hardly recognize the new landscape, which is now filled with groups with strange names—Pharisees, Sadducees, and Zealots. Roman soldiers are at the center of things, and we begin to encounter Greek culture.

What has happened during these four hundred years?

GREEKS BEARING GIFTS

As Israel's glory dimmed, other nations began to shine brightly. First among the rising powers was Greece. Out of fear of the Persians, Philip of Macedon began to gather a confederation of regions and city-states that became an imposing Greek alliance. When he was assassinated, his teenage son took the throne; we know him today as Alexander the Great.

Alexander was no timid youngster. He was actually more ambitious and aggressive than his father, and he set out to obliterate Persia, which was the current regional power. His troops pushed into western Asia, defeated Persia, and, just afterward, took control of Palestine as well. The year was 332 BC.

We can imagine Alexander and his war machine approaching Jerusalem. The Jews knew a conquering army when they saw one. This could be another Assyria or Babylon. Word had spread. This army was known to have routed the Persians and recently triumphed at Gaza. The Judeans could only anticipate the worst. Gathering to discuss their options, they decided the only thing to do was to make terms and find out the price of peace. So the high priest, we're told, led a delegation to ride out and meet Alexander.

Whatever actually happened, the Greeks proved to be more reasonable than expected. The ancient historian Josephus claims Alexander entered the temple and made a sacrifice to honor the God of Abraham, Isaac, and Jacob. But this is likely to be a mere legend. The truth is, Alexander wasn't interested in challenging a nation's religious practices. The Jews could have their temple, their priests, their sacrifices. What the Greeks imposed was their culture. They believed that while armies win battles, languages and customs win hearts and minds. The key to a stable empire was common practices among far-flung regions.

For example, Alexander encouraged Jews to emigrate to Egypt and elsewhere,[8] and people from those nations to come to Palestine. He founded new Greek cities in the lands he took over. Over the years, the Mediterranean world forged new connections it hadn't had in the past. Travel became more common.

The Greek language was the key to all of it. *Koine* or common Greek was the tongue of the empire, to the point that Jewish parents worried about their children losing their Hebrew language and the many ideas and principles that came with it, including spiritual principles.

During this period, synagogues became more common. While the temple was primarily a place of worship, synagogues were places in the villages where the Scriptures could be read and discussed, prayers could be offered, children could be taught, and perhaps a bit of gossip could be exchanged.

In the past, the presence of God had solely been associated with the tabernacle and the temple in Jerusalem. But now it was painfully established that temples could be destroyed, and Jerusalem might be too distant for travel anyway. Synagogues presented a workable solution, but they also began a shift in Judaism from a centralized religion of public sacrifice to one of local gathering, study, and prayer.

THE SEPTUAGINT

Another result of the *Hellenization* or spread of Greek culture in the Jewish world was that the Septuagint came into being. This was

8. "332 B.C.E. Alexander the Great," Center for Online Judaic Studies, accessed May 16, 2023, cojs.org/332-b-c-e-alexander-great. Quoting Joseph M. Modrzejewski, *The Jews of Egypt: From Rameses II to Emperor Hadrian* (Princeton, NJ: Princeton University Press, 1997).

the most important of all Bible translations because it liberated the Word of God from the confines of the Hebrew language. Now the Scriptures roamed freely in what was now the common tongue of a wide-ranging empire.

The backstory of the Septuagint (Greek for "the seventy") is another matter of cherished legend. Ptolemy II Philadelphus, the Greek Pharaoh of Egypt, decided to gather all the books of the world into his great library. He wrote to the Jewish high priest and asked him to send learned men to Alexandria to translate the Hebrew Scriptures into Greek. Seventy-two were dispatched—six from each of the twelve tribes of Israel. Each one entered a chamber by himself, and after seventy-two days, their translations were made, completely from memory, and found to be identical! This proved the power of God to those who found this story credible.

We have the account from a document known as the Letter of Aristeas, apparently written at least a century later. What we can know for certain, however, is that by now, Jewish communities were spread across the Mediterranean region. Many had fled during the invasions of Assyria and Babylon, and this outflow of God's people, known as the *Diaspora*, continued in waves up to and after the time the Second Temple was destroyed in AD 70.

As time passed, even in Palestine, fewer and fewer were literate in written Hebrew, but many knew Greek. The books of Moses were slowly becoming archaic and unfamiliar, so the appearance of the Septuagint was a boon to those who longed to read the books of the Law and share them with their children. The Hebrew Scriptures could be read not only by Jews but by people of other nations.

The translation remained highly respected for centuries; its symbol was LXX—seventy in Roman numerals. At first, the Septuagint contained only the first five books of our Old Testament, the books of Moses. In time, however, the rest of the books were included, so that today, the term *Septuagint* is actually used for the entire Old Testament Greek translation. Most of the New

Testament's Old Testament quotes come from Septuagint rather than the original Hebrew. It was the Bible of that period.

But the Old Testament we use today is translated from Hebrew, the original language, and not from the Septuagint. There are certain differences between our translations and the one made two thousand years ago. For example, the Septuagint version of Jeremiah is almost 20 percent shorter than our version. This was puzzling until the Dead Sea Scrolls were discovered in the 1940s, and a similarly shorter version of Jeremiah was among the findings. This confirms there were slight variations in the Old Testament Scriptures of that period, though impressively few.

POWER STRUGGLE

Alexander the Great died at the age of thirty-two in 323 BC. The cause of death is uncertain, but he is said to have collapsed in Babylon, in the palace of Nebuchadnezzar, a later ruler than the one found in the book of Daniel.

Who could replace such a striking figure as the Greek commander? There was no plan of succession, and as a result, five generals from different regions divvied up the empire. In some regions, it worked well; in Palestine, it didn't. Two of the generals, Ptolemy and Antigonus, struggled over control of Palestine. For many years, there was no true ruler. It came to a battle in 301 BC, when Antigonus was killed. Yet for various reasons, there was still no agreement on who should rule Palestine. For the Jews, it was somewhat like being caught in a long custody fight. Even so, they fared quite well, able to live and worship as they pleased, even as Greek ways and practices began to dominate daily life.

The relative peace was not to last. For one thing, the office of high priest was politicized under Greek rule. It had been a lifetime position, but various ambitious men began to offer bribes as they sought the important post.

In 175, Antiochus IV, known as Antiochus Epiphanes, became king of what was now known as the Seleucid Empire. Seleucus was one of Alexander's generals, but the Seleucid Empire was mostly in Western Asia. In time, the rulers referred to themselves as Syrian kings, with Antioch as their capital.

Antiochus Epiphanes was an unpredictable despot. Behind his back, he was known as Epimenes—"insane." He had been raised in Rome as a hostage in one of his father's disputes. During his time as ruler, relations between Greeks and Jews grew much more tense. Among other reasons, there was more awareness and discomfort with the growing Greek influence and the loss of identity as God's chosen people. Even some Jewish priests were pro-Hellenist by this time, and the cultural tensions were coming to a head. People also objected to the corruption of the office of high priest.

But Antiochus's attention was on Egypt, where he wanted to gain control. The Romans were already there, however—their star was rising now—and when Antiochus showed up in Alexandria, he was commanded to leave. He couldn't have been in a good mood as he came home to Jerusalem only to learn that his appointed priest, who had purchased the office, had been driven out.

Antiochus flew into a rage. He commanded his soldiers to kill great numbers of Jews and finish this troublesome monotheistic religion once and for all.

To show he meant business, Antiochus entered the temple and sacrificed a pig on the altar. For the Jews, this was an unthinkable blasphemy. Antiochus also ordered the burning of any copies of the Hebrew Scriptures and withdrew many religious freedoms, such as the circumcision of boys and the observance of the Sabbath. He grossly underestimated the reaction he would create.

A FLEETING TASTE OF FREEDOM

Naturally, the Jews were devastated. They hadn't anticipated this wave of terror just because they rejected a dishonest high priest. At first, uncertain of how to respond, they simply complied with the commands. But then came a fresh outrage, an order that people from each town offer sacrifices to the supreme Greek god Zeus. This violated the most crucial commandments given to Moses. There is but one God, and they were to bow to no other. To do so was the most horrendous of transgressions.

In one village, a priest named Mattathias was selected to offer his sacrifice to Zeus. When he refused and a younger man stepped up to offer the sacrifice instead, Mattathias killed the young Jew as well as the Greek officer who had made the demand. Mattathius knew he'd placed his entire family in grave danger, so he took his five sons and a few other supporters and went into hiding.

The third son, Judas, became the leader of this resistance. He became known as "the hammerer" (*Maccabeus*) because he struck powerfully and surely—a new Gideon who could fight cleverly against larger armies. Soldiers came flocking to join the new army, enflamed by the hope of freedom and the urgency of saving Judaism.

More importantly, Antiochus was distracted by greater problems. His troops were busy dealing with crises in other regions, so he sent fewer soldiers to put down the Jewish revolt.

The Judeans must have been surprised by the ease of their success, for they gained control of Jerusalem after a mere three years of skirmishes. It was a proud moment for the Jewish people. The temple was purified once again, and the time of victory was memorialized in what is today celebrated as Hanukkah.

Judas Maccabeus began to think in broader terms: full independence for the people of God! Seeking sweet autonomy such as the Jews hadn't enjoyed for generations, he established a friendly relationship with Rome as a political boost, but then died in battle in 160 BC. He was replaced by his brother Jonathan, who wasn't the field general Judas had been and thus began to lose power. Eventually he made a deal with one of the Seleucids—purportedly a son of Antiochus—and supported him in exchange for the office of high priest. The struggle

with the Seleucids had come full circle, so that the Maccabee movement lost a bit of the moral high ground it had occupied.

Still, the war continued. One more of Mattathias's sons, Simon,
finally secured Jewish freedom from taxation in 141 BC. He, too,
served in the odd combination of high priest and field general; at this
point, the office became a matter of inheritance.

This marked the beginning of the Hasmonean dynasty, established by the same sons of Mattathias. *Hasmonean* was simply a form
of the name Asmoneus, an ancestor of Mattathias. But the successors
of Judas Maccabeus were now priestly and referring to themselves as
kings.

They ruled politically for about eighty years as the Seleucids
grew ever weaker. In such a time, it was possible for the Hasmoneans
to actually extend the footprint of the Jewish nation, such as it was, in
surrounding territories such as Samaria. But they were beginning to
rule like the Seleucids they had overcome; for example, they destroyed
the Samaritan temple at Mount Gerizim and forced Judaism on some
of the lands they occupied.

There was also a great deal of violence and mutiny within the
ruling family. Aristobulus I, for example, imprisoned his mother,
who starved to death. He also imprisoned three of his brothers, kill-
ing one of them. The people who had lifted up Judas Maccabeus as a
hero now became restless under what had become a line of leaders as
uninspiring as their forebears.

Yet there were rumors of a new empire from far to the west in
Rome that was growing in power all the time. The Roman Republic
had a presence in Egypt, Syria, and elsewhere. Sooner or later,
wouldn't its troops show up in Palestine? All the previous empires
had done so.

PHARISEES, SADDUCEES, AND ESSENES

All the changes in this part of the world were being imposed
from the outside—first from Greece, then from Syria through the

Seleucids. People were now speaking and writing the Greek language; Hasmonean rulers were working with the Seleucids and sometimes the Romans. The great days of the faith's fathers—Abraham, Moses, David, and Elijah—seemed distant, although rabbinic teaching continued. The Jewish world, once fairly secluded, was becoming international in ways that challenged the understanding of the Mosaic law, which seemed to indicate that God's chosen people were special and separate.

What sense of all this could be made from a spiritual point of view?

That question resulted in a great many changes to established Judaism, highlighted by various factions that came into being. What was the place of the temple, which had been defiled and later purified? For many, it was more important than ever, particularly for those living in or near Jerusalem. It became not only a religious center but a place where many other social activities occurred, much like the medieval cathedral or the Christian church in general during many eras.

An order later known as the Sadducees had taken form among the temple crowd. Some, but not all, were priests. Largely, these were aristocratic, politically connected leaders who operated the various offices of the temple. They profited, for example, from the sale of animals for sacrifice.

The Sadducees believed only in the written law that was contained in the Torah. To expand upon it or provide new interpretations was to present troublesome challenges, and the Sadducees wanted no such thing. They didn't believe in any form of afterlife because the Books of Moses said nothing about that. Being well-to-do, the Sadducees were in favor of Hellenistic influences and the status quo in general. They were comfortable, so why rock the boat? The Sadducees faded away after the temple was destroyed in AD 70, during the early Christian era, but they were a fairly important group during the intertestamental period and the time of Jesus.

Less tied to the temple were the Pharisees, who comprised more of a working-class movement and were often associated with the new synagogues. The Pharisees believed not only in the written law, but oral tradition as well—thinking that God expounded to Moses on the law in greater detail than the scrolls revealed, and these extra explanations made up the traditional interpretations that had been passed down. These were eventually written down as the Talmud, a vast body of more than six thousand modern pages that the Pharisees attempted to master and enforce.

Everyone knew there must be Sabbath rest, for example, but what constituted work that would violate that? The Pharisees had detailed examples and solutions. During these Hellenistic times, people had generally grown lax toward obedience to the law and ritual purity; the Pharisees represented a reaction (perhaps an overreaction) to that laxity. They hated Greek influences and wanted to bring back what they understood as the *old-time religion* of their forefathers.

Then there were the Essenes, who saw neither the temple nor the synagogue as places to find refuge; their idea was to drop out. The Essenes saw the Sadducees as too worldly and the Pharisees as too legalistic. The answer, they felt, was in mysticism, self-denial (asceticism), voluntary poverty, and the renunciation of wealth and property.[9] Some lived in small communes in populated areas, but it also seems that a few Essene groups may have created their own monastic-type refuges away from the cities.

In 1947, a shepherd who was looking for a stray sheep tossed a rock into a cave in a desolate area near the West Bank, and he heard an odd ping from one of the stones he'd thrown. When he investigated, he discovered seven scrolls in clay jars. When the find was made public, it created a sensation. More caves were located, and the result was a large library associated with an Essene community from around the time of Christ. We know this library as the Dead Sea Scrolls.

---

9. D. K. Falk, "Essenes," in *New Bible Dictionary*, ed. D. R. W. Wood et al. (Leicester, England; Downers Grove, IL: InterVarsity Press, 1996), 340.

A few of the documents were biblical; for instance, there was a nearly complete version of Isaiah. The diverse collection of scrolls was an archaeological bonanza. More than one thousand manuscripts were eventually discovered, and some believe that these included pieces from the collection of the Second Temple itself, stowed in caves for safekeeping during times of attack and persecution.

The Jewish historian Josephus named the Pharisees, the Sadducees, and the Essenes as the three primary directions of the Jewish faith during the Second Temple period. One found meaning in ritual purity, attained through fanatical adherence to the law; another found it in temple fellowship and political pragmatism; and the third found it in mystical piety.

Who was left out? The answer: a great number of Jews who couldn't identify with any of these options. They struggled to survive, to pay taxes to their conquering overlords, and to find whatever meaning they could in everyday life. The well-off Sadducees looked down upon them. The Pharisees looked for sin among them to call out and condemn. The Essenes—well, they were just strange and distant. And the high priests were Seleucid puppets.[10]

Faith in the likelihood of God doing something new and wonderful was fading, but some of the common people remembered the old prophecies that called for a new King David, a messiah who would restore the lost glory of Israel.

However, those were the words of chattering, pious prophets, and where were such men now? The prophets had fallen silent for four hundred years, and no one had come forth since Malachi. Through crisis after crisis, there had been no prophets, no miracles of God.

THE BOOKS FROM "BETWEEN"

While no prophets were forthcoming, the writers of the Judean hills and plains were as active as ever. There were a great many books

10. Rabbi Leibel Gniwisch, "The High Priest in Jewish Tradition," Chabad-Lubavitch Media Center, accessed May 16, 2023, www.chabad.org/library/article_cdo/aid/4195084/jewish/The-High-Priest-in-Jewish-Tradition.htm#High.

written in the four centuries between the Old and New Testaments. Today they're known as the Apocrypha in Protestant churches. Although they are not considered the inspired Word of God, they are still worthy of reading and study.

Some Bibles contain these books, as did the Septuagint and the 1611 King James Version of the Bible. The Roman Catholic and Eastern Orthodox churches include certain of these books with their editions of Scripture and term them *deuterocanonical* literature, meaning "belonging to the second canon." While early Christians used and quoted from these books, references to them in the New Testament are rare. For example, Jude 1:14–15 quotes from 1 Enoch, just as Paul quotes Greek poets.

The collection of about twenty deuterocanonical books is random and not a group intended as a set. Most of them were written during the period when the canon of our Old Testament was closing—that is, becoming recognized as complete and no longer open to additions. Yet these books can be very useful for historical context, comparison, and insight into the canonical books.

For example, 1 and 2 Maccabees tell us the story of the Jewish rebellion led by Judas Maccabeus. They cover the persecution of Antiochus Epiphanes, the revolt and early victories against the Seleucids, the recapture of Jerusalem, and the purification of the temple. These are basic texts for the Jewish celebration of Hannukah. Several of the books, such as Tobit and Judith, offer glimpses into the faith of the Jewish prisoners in exile.

Some books are additions to canonical material. Bel and the Dragon is a fascinating extra tale of Daniel, who demonstrates to King Cyrus the foolishness of Babylonian religions. In one case, Daniel challenges Cyrus to a test to prove an idol of the god Bel does not eat the food offerings left for it. He reveals the deception by which priests have been stealing in to eat the food and make it appear that the statue did so. In another story, Daniel slays the dragon worshiped by the Babylonians by feeding it hot cakes that explode inside the dragon's stomach after being consumed. This is actually one of four additions to our biblical book of Daniel.

There is also a letter from Jeremiah and a book of Baruch, who was Jeremiah's personal secretary and assistant. Sirach is like a latter-day book of Proverbs, with ethical teaching written in verse. The Wisdom of Solomon is a similar collection. There is also Psalm 151, found in the Septuagint but not in the canonical book of Psalms, which stop at number 150. The Prayer of Manasseh is a king's prayer of repentance in Babylon, while 1 and 2 Esdras are grab-bags of tales, wisdom, and apocalypse.

The apocryphal works make for fascinating reading, though less essential than biblical Scripture. They also help to fill in that great, four-century gap between the Old and New Testaments.

THE ROMANS ARRIVE

This same period of time, the second half of the intertestamental period, saw the emergence of the Roman Empire, though it wouldn't reach full power and size until AD 117. At one point, there had been a friendly agreement between the Jews and the Romans, who supported the former's resistance to the Seleucids, the Romans' rivals.

From 73 to 63 BC, the Romans were attempting to take full control of the eastern shores of the Mediterranean Sea. The last of the Seleucids were being driven out. Pompey led the conquest of an area that included Palestine, a conquest completed in 63 BC. This was thirty-two years before what is considered to be the dawn of the age of Imperial Rome. Julius Caesar, the great military leader, had only been born one year earlier.

Rome had come to Palestine at the right time. A civil war had broken out there, with two Hasmonean rivals struggling for power. Pompey chose a side and helped to install that leader as ruler and high priest, but there was a price to pay. Judea would now be a client state, subservient to the Romans.

It was just the beginning.

This arrangement lasted through the reign of Herod the Great (37–34 BC). Herod was intensely loyal to the Romans, cooperating in every way. When he died, the emperor Augustus, the first Roman emperor, divided Judea into three smaller principalities—Judea, Galilee, and Batanea, also known as Bashan—and gave each to a son to rule. But this system didn't prove to be workable, and in the year AD 6, Rome annexed Judea and began using short-term governors, one of whom was Pontius Pilate. Judea became the catch-all name for the region, including some land beyond the Jordan River. To the north, beyond the region of Samaria, was Galilee, where Nazareth was found. To the west were Perea and Decapolis.

The Judeans themselves surely noticed that a new era had arrived. While they'd had various levels of autonomy in recent centuries, the Romans were far more present, more oppressive, and more demanding. They had two interests: peace and tax collections.

This was the setting when, sometime during the final years of Herod the Great, a census was declared to organize the paying of taxes.

> *And it came to pass in those days, that there went out a decree from Caesar Augustus that all the world should be taxed.*
>
> (Luke 2:1 KJV)

The Judeans were correct: a new era was indeed dawning upon the world. Yet no one would have expected it to involve a young couple trudging toward Bethlehem in the final days of this period, on their way to be counted.

5

LETTERS OF HOPE
AND PROMISE

The general had a wife named Thessalonica. To please her, he named a Mediterranean coastal town after her in 316 BC.

The general, whose own name was Cassander, served under Alexander the Great. The area in question was a loose group of smaller villages, pulled together to become a major port city that would flourish long after Alexander and his armies had scattered with the dust of history.

The thriving city of Thessalonica was in Macedonia, north of Greece, though today it is Greece's second largest city. It has been consistently occupied since Cassander honored his wife. The city was beginning to come into its own just before the time of Christ. When Julius Caesar was assassinated, Thessalonica's ruling council backed the right parties in distant Italy, and the result was that Mark Antony granted Thessalonica its self-rule as a city. In the Roman Empire, that was a highly treasured right.

Thessalonica had miles of coastline to serve as harbors. This, along with the Roman roads and the Greek language, helped the city prosper as the Roman Empire did the same. Like many such places, it was a melting pot of cultures and faiths, including a synagogue for Jewish settlers and travelers, and open areas where street-corner philosophers debated their views of the cosmos.

In AD 50, three travelers trudged into town, entering by the Apollonia road on the east side. There was nothing remarkable about them, though people noticed that one of them did most of the talking while the other two provided support.

The men first attracted notice at the synagogue, where it quickly became obvious that they were very cerebral Jews—at least the talkative visitor was. He had no interest in chatting about local gossip or politics. He changed the subject to the laws and the prophets at every opportunity, and he seemed to carry in-depth knowledge of his subject.

Offering his name as Paul of Tarsus, the man pointed mostly to the messianic prophecies and ideas of sin and impurity. But his commentary on all of this was eye-opening, to say the least.

The following Sabbath—and the Sabbath after that—the man was back, building on his arguments to mixed results. For one thing, attendance was way up. The trio had made some friends by this time and was attracting a crowd. Listeners were hanging on to Paul's every word, and they'd brought friends of their own.

But the speaker had made some enemies too, and these had also gathered a few friends: a mob of ruffians from the street. The synagogue of Thessalonica had never seen such tension. Normally it was a calm place for Jewish fellowship, quiet discussion, and prayer. Now it seemed as though a riot might break out.

The city had a popular temple to Caesar. Emperor worship was one of the chief factors that kept Thessalonica in good standing with Rome—self-rule, lower taxes. The local Jews worshiped their own God, but they usually did it with no controversy whatsoever. Paul and his two companions were threatening that peace. They had actually started a small group for fellowship and worship—an *ekklesia*— totally committed to the idea that the Messiah, the Christ, had come to earth, and that everyone, not just Jews, needed to serve Him.

This new Jewish sect freely admitted that Jesus of Nazareth, their leader and even their God, had been crucified by Rome as a common criminal. Many questioned the idea of a crucified God. This Messiah had been rejected by His own people in Jerusalem. In every conceivable way, it was the worst idea for a new religion anyone could have imagined. But the fact that Rome had stepped in to quench the movement in Jerusalem made it a nonstarter in Thessalonica.

Still, here were Paul and his friends, Silas and Timothy, making converts. No wonder the locals accused them of turning the world upside down.

The mob began searching for the three men but could only round up Jason, one of the local enthusiasts who had championed the visitors. His house was attacked, but the trio had been smuggled out of town by night. Rid of these troublemakers, the peace was restored.

The trio was next heard from in Beroea, where they were up to their old tricks, spreading their crazy message. The Thessalonica mob regathered and actually pursued them there. The main inciter, Paul, had set off for Athens by this time, though his two assistants were still around. These events are recorded in Acts 17.

People all over began to hear word of this new message, which was catching on in the biggest cities. Paul was quite intentional about selecting key metropolitan centers for new churches. Thessalonica, for example, was not only a major port city but was also located by a key Roman highway. Such locations would encourage a new faith to go "viral," as it were, with people becoming excited in town and then spreading the message by land and sea.

Not long afterward, Paul, Silas, and Timothy together wrote a letter to their friends in Thessalonica, who seemed to be losing some of their enthusiasm. Paul set forth to remind them that Jesus would be returning. He also reminded them of the essentials of the new faith.

The letter was cherished as the church grew. We remember the first letter to the Thessalonians now as a critically important part of our Bible. By most calculations, it was the first written words of the New Testament. It's significant that it's a letter from three men rather than one. Paul's writing career had only just begun.

It seems counterintuitive that the letters we find in the Bible after the book of Acts were written before the four gospels that tell the story of Jesus. Since the gospels of Matthew, Mark, Luke, and John describe activities from years earlier, they are positioned at the front of our New Testament. Paul was converted just after the resurrection of Jesus, at the point where the Gospels end. (See Acts 9:1–6.) So how is it that these biographies of Jesus weren't written until after Paul's first letter to the Thessalonians—and all of his other letters?

The top priority of the early Christians was probably not to write things down. The *gospel* (good news) was urgent, even revolutionary. It was, in fact, a current event. The first Christians had known Jesus and seen His activities firsthand. The new, established church was a Jerusalem phenomenon anyway. It was made up of the apostles, other disciples, and people who were flocking to be a part of the movement after hearing word-of-mouth about the miracles. The gospel was new and fresh, and the attention of Christians was on the here and now, not on writing down facts and ideas for posterity. Most of us, in fact, live with the same *carpe diem* attitude. We seize the day and give little thought about tomorrow.

The Way, as the Jesus movement was called, carried plenty of adrenalin, but it wasn't stress-free. There was persecution from the Jewish establishment, and the resulting commotion made the church a Roman headache as well. Some new believers fled to nearby cities such as Antioch, where there were large Jewish populations open to hearing the gospel message. But few in these new centers had witnessed the key events. The story and teachings of Jesus were strange and fascinating, but much less familiar.

When Paul and his friends began to push for intentional mission journeys to win converts among the gentiles, there was a greater need for information and particularly for leadership. Paul sent his young protégé Timothy back to Thessalonica to help the young church, but he also felt the need to write a letter of encouragement. He understood that a letter held the advantage of permanence since it could be saved for future reference. He later wrote the Thessalonians a second letter.

This is how, twenty years before the first gospel was written, a handful of instructional letters began to circulate, to be copied and saved, and ultimately to be afforded supreme authority as the inspired Word of God.

THE APOSTLE AND THE EPISTLES

There are other letters in the New Testament from John, Peter, James, and Jude, and even an anonymous letter to the Hebrews. These *epistles* (Greek for letters) provide invaluable glimpses into the early church, its challenges, and its interests. When they were written by apostles, the closest disciples of Christ, they held greater weight in early Christianity and were far more likely to be preserved and considered authoritative.

Questions arose: What should we believe about this, or how should we handle that? Since Jesus left behind no writings, the letters of the apostles and early Christian leaders such as James were needed that much more. Paul's letters were held in particularly high esteem.

Paul was a special case. He never walked with Jesus, heard Him teach, or saw a miracle other than the one by which he himself was converted. According to Acts, he was involved with the earliest days of the new Christian church, but only in a negative way: he persecuted Christians with the same zeal he later exhibited in ministering to them.

But by virtue of his supernatural encounter with the resurrected Jesus on the road to Damascus, he counted himself as an apostle, and the first Christians confirmed his standing, especially after a momentous trip to Jerusalem, when he spent time with James and Peter, the leaders of the Christian movement. The power of Paul's ministry and passion for missions brought him quick acceptance as a Christian leader wherever churches were forming. He founded many of them himself.

Each writer of a New Testament letter has his own particular style. But Paul's letters receive special attention because they offer our earliest snapshot of Christian life, they're beautifully written and argued, and they offer the basic architecture of the Christian faith, both then and now.

Paul wrote his letters in Greek and in the Hellenist form of the time. This meant he used a particular structure that we also find in countless other surviving letters from the era. This meant beginning with an identification and description, usually "Paul, an apostle," and a further description of his role as a Christian. Just the identifier offered valuable information about the faith:

Paul, a bondservant of Jesus Christ, called to be an apostle, sepa-
rated to the gospel of God which He promised before through His
prophets in the Holy Scriptures.   (Romans 1:1–2)

In general, an identification of the recipient follows.

To all the saints in Christ Jesus who are in Philippi, with the
bishops and deacons.   (Philippians 1:1)

In the Greek style, a greeting came next. Paul liked using, "Grace and peace." The former was the preferred Hellenistic greeting, while "peace" (*shalom*) was the common Jewish greeting. This form might also mention the carrier who brought the letter.

What followed was the body of the letter, which was much more personal and individual, but still used certain rules of composition, particularly when teaching. Paul used Greek rhetorical techniques. He had been trained in Jewish rhetoric and debate as a Pharisee, under the legendary Gamaliel, but he was also fluent in Greek thinking, and his mind was well-organized and quick.

In the book of Acts, Paul defends himself before the Roman governor Felix and makes his case effectively. (See Acts 24:10–21.) Whether in person or on parchment, he was able to lodge an effective argument, using rhetorical devices that would appeal to whomever the listener might be. Quite often, Paul was on the attack against his critics or spreaders of heresy, and he'd use his letters to offer reasoning that shut down whatever he saw as the threat.

Yet his letters often show a great deal of warmth and love for his recipients. He tended to close with personal messages for his friends in the churches. Paul was as comfortable talking to ordinary believers as he was high government bureaucrats or Athenian philosophers.

The whole complex, charismatic personality of Paul comes across in his letters to the churches—his passion for Christ, his love for his brothers and sisters in Christ, his intolerance of disunity and disruption, and especially his limitless energy to visit more places and see more people become followers of Jesus Christ.

Some of Paul's letters are quite short and compact. Philemon is a letter addressed only to the man of that name. It's 335 Greek words long and is an appeal for the recipient to welcome Onesimus, a runaway slave. Yet Romans, his lengthiest and weightiest letter, offers the most substantial and fully developed Christian theology of the early church. This is why it was placed in front of all the other epistles in the New Testament, just after the Gospels and Acts. It's a full explanation of the nature and inescapability of sin, the death sentence human sin imposes, and the hopelessness of humanity atoning for it through any human means. As a result, the Jewish system of sacrifice is inadequate. Any number of good works will fall far short.

Salvation, Paul argues, comes solely from the grace of God and is achieved through faith in the atoning work of Jesus in His crucifixion and subsequent victory over death in His resurrection.

ARCHITECT AND POET

Paul's letter to the Romans is more than a theological treatise, however. It carries the full power of the apostle's inspired literary gifts. The eighth chapter of the book, in particular, not only teaches, but also inspires through poetry that has lost none of its strength through centuries of translations into various languages:

Yet in all these things we are more than conquerors through Him who loved us. For I am persuaded that neither death nor life, nor angels nor principalities nor powers, nor things present nor things to come, nor height nor depth, nor any other created thing, shall be able to separate us from the love of God which is in Christ Jesus our Lord. (Romans 8:37–39)

No wonder the writings of Paul have been the favorites of preachers for twenty centuries. Power and energy crackle through every paragraph; as we read them, we find power and passion that are infectious. In Romans, Paul explains how Christianity works, but he also demonstrates how it *feels*. It's like having the mechanics of an automobile explained, complete with schematic charts, and then being taken for a ride in a fine car on a lovely spring day. Paul the apostle speaks to the mind and the heart. He is the architect of early Christian theology, but also the poet who provides its music for the soul. No writer has had a more profound effect on the world.

His theological architecture has inspired debate over the years. Skeptics step forward to accuse Paul of inventing Christianity all by himself. Jesus, they say, was a fine ethical teacher who taught people to love one another and talked constantly about the kingdom of God. It was Paul, coming along later, who worked out theories of justification by faith, substitutionary atonement, and the like. While Paul was in love with abstract theory, Jesus talked about everyday issues.

On its face, this argument is understandable to a certain extent. But it ignores the context of both forms of writing. Jesus is the subject of four biographies called the Gospels, which describe His movements and a sampling of His teaching. He spoke the Aramaic form of Hebrew and lived in a Jewish world, with a few encounters with gentiles. Paul's letters come from gentile environments, concern specific churches and their problems, and set out to explain Jewish thought and Christ's fulfillment of it. It's true that Jesus focused on the coming of the kingdom of God, and Paul used different language and rhetorical approaches. But the two spoke in different genres to different audiences. What actually stands out is the lack of *disagreement*.

If Jesus and Paul were in conflict, surely it would become evident somewhere in the New Testament. Yet the emphases of the two fit together snugly.

Trained as a Pharisee, Paul had a language and outlook that was steeped in the Mosaic law, the issue of purity, and the need for sacrifice. He viewed Jesus through that lens and brilliantly demonstrated how Jesus was the ultimate once-for-all sacrifice. Jesus would have taken no issue with that stance; He said that He came *"to give His life [as] a ransom for many"* (Matthew 20:28). And the ethical teachings of Jesus are present in all of the passages in which Paul teaches us to bear with one another, love unconditionally, and avoid self-righteous hypocrisy. Both men passionately preached the need to take the gospel to the whole world.

When Paul's epistles and the teachings of Jesus are seen together, they suggest no division, but instead offer a complete and satisfying picture of one consistent faith. We have the writings of the first generations of apostolic fathers to demonstrate that the Gospels and Paul's letters were both considered inspired and worthy as Scripture given to guide Christian beliefs.

THE OTHER EPISTLES

Not only is the selection of New Testament books important, their order is also telling. The Gospels are placed first, though written after Paul's letters, because the story of Jesus is essential. It all begins there.

Acts comes next, as a continuation of the gospel story. Then come the letters of Paul because they were considered by early Christians to be preeminent among the letters, packed, as they are, with basic Christian teaching. Among these, Romans holds the leadoff position because of the sheer density and magnitude of its particular teaching.

The New Testament is front-loaded in that way, with the early church's highest-trafficked books in the front and the later, less-affirmed books toward the back. This isn't in any way to suggest a lower degree of divine inspiration for the final books because there are no degrees of that. Over the centuries, various books have been rediscovered or reevaluated. Early Christianity set the table of contents, and it has remained in the given order.

The Pastoral Epistles (1 and 2 Timothy and Titus) seem to come toward the latter years of Paul's ministry and bear a different style. The authorship of Hebrews is uncertain, and apostolic authorship was an important credential. As a matter of fact, the German reformer Martin Luther, whose actions set off the Protestant Reformation, considered Hebrews, James, Jude, and Revelation to be somewhat sketchy as additions to the canon of Scripture.

Luther called James's letter an "epistle of straw." Yet this very letter is highly valued by Bible readers today for its practical, everyday advice, whereas Luther much preferred the theological intricacies of Paul's work. As a matter of fact, some scholars now believe that James, said to be a half-brother of Jesus—although he identifies himself as *a bondservant of God and of the Lord Jesus Christ*" (James 1:1)—wrote his letter around AD 50, about the same time Paul, Silas, and Timothy were dispatching their first letter to the Thessalonians. Given deep study, we begin to see that James's letter bears a close relationship to Jesus's Sermon on the Mount.

One would expect Peter's two letters and John's three letters to be found much sooner in the New Testament. These are surely the most beloved two disciples—the pair who engaged in a footrace to the empty tomb. (See John 20:3–4.) Their letters are filled with favorite passages, but their authorship was less certain in the early church. Certainly John's letters are written in the same warm style as his gospel. Peter, whom tradition connects to the church in Rome, writes about faith in times of persecution. Early Christians revered all five of these letters, and they earned a place in the canon, where we still attribute them to the traditional authors.

Finally, Revelation stands alone. It's an *apocalyptic* work, which places it in a specific genre of literature that flourished from about 200 BC to AD 200. Revelation uses a series of symbolic visions to describe the coming judgment of God, the salvation of the saints, the punishment of evil rulers, and the end of earthly time. Simultaneously, it speaks to the persecution of Christians during the time in which it was written: the reigns of the emperors Nero and Domitian. In the Old Testament, the book of Daniel is an example of apocalyptic literature.

Again, there were some in the first two centuries who questioned the inclusion of Revelation among the other New Testament Scriptures. On the other hand, it was a very popular book, discussed and studied quite often. Its letters to the seven churches are still frequently read and used as sermon topics, even if the symbolism and obscurity of much of the rest of the book is difficult to puzzle out. (See Revelation 2:1–3:22.)

THE FIRST-CENTURY BIBLE

To peruse the letters of the New Testament is to walk among a gold mine of spiritual treasure. Yet it's important to remember that these books weren't originally recognized as the same timeless, divine authority we see them as now. Scripture for the early Christians was our Old Testament. Jesus quoted from the Law and the Prophets. On the day of Pentecost, Peter's sermon text was taken from the book of Joel. And even in these first-century letters, the Old Testament writings are always front and center. During the first generation of Christianity, the beloved older Scriptures still provided the foundation and authority for preaching and study. They were not seen as surpassed, but were recognized as more relevant than ever—their promises had finally been carried out. The messianic prophecies had been proven true, and God's various covenants had found their ultimate expression. Jesus said, *"Do not think that I have come to abolish the Law or the Prophets; I have not come to abolish them but to fulfill them"* (Matthew 5:17 NIV).

What was new was the opportunity to show the fulfillment of the Scriptures through the coming of Jesus. Christians have never discarded the books of the Old Testament because neither Jesus nor the first Christians did any such thing. They saw a perfect continuity between what God spoke to the prophets, and what He manifested in their own time.

How, then, did they see the letters of Paul, John, Peter, and the others? These were looked upon as contemporary commentaries on what God had done in reference to past revelation. Even so, they were seen immediately as carrying the full authority of the apostles, who were granted that stature by Christ. Paul stated and defended his authority as coming from heaven. These writings were considered invaluable, so they were preserved, read, and quoted repeatedly as they were in later years. As various heresies appeared, the New Testament letters, along with the Gospels, were effectively appealed to for correction and the final word.

As we'll see, time and the efficacy of these letters transformed them from contemporary reading material to full recognition, within a few generations, that these were divinely inspired writings— Scripture worthy to share space with the equally time-honored books of Genesis through Malachi.

Paul, Silas, and Timothy, who wrote to the Thessalonians, couldn't have imagined that their personal letters, scribbled in spare moments on parchment and carried off by messenger, would shape the world and hundreds of millions of followers of Christ for twenty centuries. The fact that they have done so, with no flaw or blemish becoming evident in them, only confirms that these were compositions coming from somewhere much deeper and wiser than the hearts and minds of mortal writers.

6

FOUR PORTRAITS, ONE SAVIOR

Hierapolis was a Greek settlement, then a Roman city, and then a Turkish city. During Paul's life, a church flourished there. (See Colossians 4:13.) Like many of the churches in Asia Minor, which were growing steadily by the decade, the Hierapolis congregation was thriving a century after the time of Christ. Churches had become more institutional by this time. Not only were there deacons as first appointed shortly after Pentecost, but there were also bishops, elders, and, in general, more structure and organization of worship and administration of the sacraments.

We can be certain that bits and pieces of worship content from the earliest years of the church exist in our New Testament writings. Not only are the Lord's Prayer and Holy Communion in evidence in the Gospels, prescribed by Jesus Himself, but there are other passages that have the sound of early creeds and hymns. The first eighteen verses of John's gospel carry a poetic rhythm: *"In the beginning was the Word, and the Word was with God, and the Word was God"* (John 1:1). Romans 1:3–4, Philippians 2:6–11, and Colossians 1:15–18 are all examples of *doctrinal poetry*. Some of these Scriptures are likely to have been used in worship; perhaps others may simply be the inspired gift of Paul's written expression. But above all things, the first Christians wanted to hear the words of Jesus Himself.

Bishop Papias of Hierapolis gathered some of them. He wrote five books under the title of *Exposition of the Sayings of the Lord*. This volume is now sadly lost to us, though bits and pieces of it survive as quotations in other Christian books of the time. We know little else about Papias or his life, but the quotations from his work that do survive are central topics of study and discussion because they give us precious and rare information about the beginnings of the four gospels—a tantalizingly small amount, but highly fascinating just the same.

Papias's century of separation from Jesus and His disciples was still a matter of three-plus generations, and many oral traditions were likely still in circulation that might not have been written down. We often know bits of information about our great-grandparents, and perhaps their parents, but at some point, we fail to pass it on, or perhaps those who follow us fail to remember it. The chain is broken, and that information is lost to time.

Living in the late first and early second century, one could have talked to aged believers who knew the disciples and perhaps even Jesus. This is, in fact, what Papias tells us. He comments that learning from books was less valuable to him than hearing from "a living and abiding voice." When he heard that someone in another city had firsthand memories to share, he was willing to travel there to hear what they could tell him. But he also names John and Ariston as first-generation disciples he'd met. This John is not thought to be John Zebedee, the beloved disciple, but another one known as John the Elder. Ariston of Smyrna and John the Elder were both known to have walked with Jesus.

Given Papias's journalistic-styled investigations, his comments on the disciples take on more weight. In particular, he tells us that when Mark wrote his gospel, he was passing on the memories of Peter, whom he presumably assisted in Rome:

> Mark, having become Peter's interpreter, wrote down accurately everything he remembered, though not in order, of the things either said or done by Christ. For he neither heard the Lord nor followed him, but afterward, as I said, followed Peter, who adapted his teachings as needed but had no intention of giving an ordered account of the Lord's sayings.[11]

---

11. Shawn J. Wilhite, "Papias," in *The Lexham Bible Dictionary*, ed. John D. Barry et al. (Bellingham, WA: Lexham Press, 2016).

This contributes to the strong tradition that Mark, who was the first to write a gospel, was a disciple of Peter, and it dovetails with modern scholarship that continues to find traces of Peter's personal, eyewitness narrative throughout Mark's book. Papias also suggests that Matthew originally wrote his gospel in the Hebrew language, a curious suggestion that some have found questionable.

These bits and pieces of ancient discussion are more than enticing to those who study the Gospels. For ever since the days of Jesus passed beyond living memory, there has been an active fascination with the four books that are our only direct source of information on the greatest life ever lived. No matter how much we learn about Jesus and His life on the earth, it's never enough. Such is the power of our fascination with the one Man who stands out above all others.

Among scholars there have been several "quests for the historical Jesus," starting with Albert Schweitzer's book on the topic in 1906. In recent years, there has been another flurry of volumes about Jesus of Nazareth in His historical context. But even for non-scholars, for those who simply read and love the Scriptures, there are so many unanswered questions. What was going on in Jesus's life between ages twelve and thirty? What was it like to know Him? How did people respond in the wake of His resurrection?

Yet for many years after His ascension, no one thought to write a gospel. The letters of the apostles and others circulated and were immediately treasured and collected. But until Mark, no one ever collected the events and teachings of Jesus's life and wrote them down. Mark's work came about thirty-five years after the events he described. Matthew and Luke followed with their own versions shortly after that, and John wrote his interpretive gospel toward the end of the first century.

How did these books come to be written?

It should be understood that there is no absolute consensus on how the Gospels were written, why, or even in what order. There are various theories, though some are held by much larger percentages of scholars than others. What follows is the most widely accepted understanding of how the authors might have assembled and published the Gospels.

IN REMEMBRANCE

The church was born on the day of Pentecost, which was a Jewish harvest festival celebrated on the fiftieth day after the Jewish Passover. In the time of Moses, death had *passed over* the Israelite babies, and the people had escaped from Egyptian slavery. Through faith in God, His people were spared. Now, the symbolism of the event had a Christian meaning—Jesus was the sacrificial lamb whose blood spared God's people.

The church became an international entity on this Christian Pentecost. A great many converts were made, and people began to praise God in their native languages. Acts 2 tells the story. It was an inversion of the Tower of Babel in the book of Genesis, when God used different languages to divide an arrogant people. (See Genesis 11:1–9.) During Pentecost, as the Holy Spirit filled the minds and hearts of the disciples and converts, these languages united people for a mission to take the gospel to every part of the earth. Of course, there was one essential language that did the lion's share of work in spreading this faith: Greek.

Even so, despite the command of Jesus to spread the gospel and the clear message of Pentecost that Christ was for *all* people, the church remained rooted in Jerusalem for its early years. The book of Acts tells us that the first believers spent much time together in the temple, fearlessly attracting new believers because of the miracles associated with them. There was a powerful sense of community, of sharing life together. Even with the persecution carried out by men like Saul of Tarsus and the martyrdom of great men such as Stephen, the faith prospered.

As believers worshiped together, they praised God, sang hymns, recited the Lord's Prayer that Jesus had taught, shared the communion meal that He had established, and repeated the stories and teachings of Jesus, particularly as new people came into the gathering, bringing their questions.

This sharing was quite important because it became the basis for the later writing of the Gospels. The first gospel was not written but spoken, as skilled orators recited the accounts and listeners absorbed them word for word.

Recent scholarship has explored the oral culture of this region. Even today, there's a powerful, relatively formal storytelling tradition in which the crowd enjoys hearing a story repeated and ensures that it's told correctly. This was reflected in first-century rabbinic culture among the Jewish people as well as other cultures of that time. The stories of Jesus would have been an important part of worship; in the beginning, they bore the contributions of people who had been involved, even people who had been healed or taught.

Traces of classic storytelling patterns can still be found in the Gospels, but these actually point more surely to accuracy rather than to the spinning of tall tales and legends. Specific names, places, and times are given; the stories being told were easily within the memory of many who had been present to witness the events. The facts were critically important in the new church: Jesus had performed signs and wonders. People had seen it with their own eyes. He had been executed, but He had come back from the dead. For this, too, there were countless witnesses. Nothing needed to be *spun*. The truth was more wonderful than any fantasy.

There were different types of stories: miracles, teachings, parables, and the stories of Jesus's trial and crucifixion. The latter stories comprise a large percentage of each of the four gospels. They are particularly sharpened by facts and detail, and there's almost no variation among them regarding how the arrest, trial, and execution are recounted. Again, this reflects the importance of these events to the early church. Pilate, the Roman procurator, is named. Caiaphas, the Jewish high priest, is named. The days and the hours are pinpointed, and small details are preserved.

During the early days of the Jerusalem church, there was a curious visitor: Saul of Tarsus, known to the Greeks and Romans as Paul. (Many Jews like Paul had two names: a Hebrew one and a Greek one.) He had represented the fiercest of threats to the church, but now he wanted, with all of his heart, to put the past behind him and become part of what he had despised and attacked. He said he had seen Christ for himself—and the evidence was in his demeanor. Paul spent several days with James, the half-brother of Jesus who now led the church, and Peter, most prominent of the disciples. Here's how Paul later describes what he learned:

> For I delivered to you first of all that which I also received: that Christ died for our sins according to the Scriptures, and that He was buried, and that He rose again the third day according to the Scriptures, and that He was seen by Cephas, then by the twelve. After that He was seen by over five hundred brethren at once, of whom the greater part remain to the present, but some have fallen asleep. After that He was seen by James, then by all the apostles.   (1 Corinthians 15:3–7)

This constitutes the first written account of the resurrection of Jesus Christ. It reads very much like the early version of a recited creed, demonstrating the manner in which the information was transmitted to Paul. The core essentials of the gospel are present: Jesus died for our sins, rose again, and many people saw it for themselves.

It's not difficult to imagine a congregation reciting those sentences, punctuated by recurring phrases such as "according to the Scriptures," and the memorable sequence of Jesus being seen in His resurrected form by one, then twelve, and then five hundred, symbolizing the exponential growth the church expected and, in fact, was experiencing.

These verses also nullify any skeptic's suggestion that the resurrection was a legend concocted long after the death of Jesus. On the first day of the Jerusalem church's existence, it was focused on a risen Lord and steeped in the facts surrounding the event.

A WRITTEN RECORD

For about a generation, the sharing of memories and their memorization by the listeners were the joy of all those who gathered together. When persecution came, people could recite these powerful stories and be reminded that Jesus was Lord.

But as time went on, there were fewer witnesses who could faithfully tell the stories. According to tradition, the apostles seemingly followed Paul's lead and vanished off into other countries for mission purposes. Jesus had not returned, as some thought He would do within a short time after His ascension to heaven.

Not only that, but the greatest growth of the church was among the gentiles, in places where Jesus had never been seen or heard. By this time, there apparently were collections of Jesus material being assembled from the oral remembrances. A crucial one would surely be the detailed account of the trial and crucifixion of Jesus. There may also have been a miracles collection: Jesus walking on the water, Jesus feeding the five thousand, and Jesus healing the daughter of Jairus. These were beloved stories people told again and again, and they simply had to be remembered.

Finally, there would have been a collection of parables and teachings. These collections, it must be emphasized, are theoretical; if they existed in parchment or codex, none have ever been seen. But gathered collections would simply be a logical transition between memory and fully compiled gospels. There is circumstantial evidence for a "sayings" collection, as we'll cover shortly. But it seems clear that the early church shared and refreshed and shared again their indelible memories of the phenomena they had seen and touched, heard and felt.

As the church grew older, more institutionalized, and more organized, it also felt a greater need for authoritative writings, written or endorsed by the apostles themselves. One of the places where this need was first acted upon may well have been Rome, the very center of the empire. There, according to several of the apostolic fathers,

Peter had come to preach and lead. Tradition also tells us that Mark, who traveled on missionary journeys with Paul and Barnabas, was close to Peter during this time. If the surviving statements of Papias of Hierapolis can be trusted, Peter recounted his memories to Mark and others around him, and Mark eventually wrote them down.

It should be noted here that the text of all four gospels is presented anonymously. The names Matthew, Mark, Luke, and John were not written on the ancient manuscripts, nor were chapter and verse numbers. All of these features were added later. But this doesn't mean the authors weren't known to the early church. All four carry ancient attestation as being the work of the authors whose names we have; this is why we place those names in our Bibles. Matthew and John are the names of disciples, while Luke and Mark were associates of Paul. The Gospels also have varying bits of evidence pointing to the named authors.

The current consensus—not universal but certainly a majority—holds that Mark was written first, in the late 60s after Jesus's death and resurrection, Matthew and Luke almost simultaneously a few years later, and John perhaps in the 90s, nearer the close of the first century. The first three, closely intertwined in their accounts, are known as the Synoptic Gospels. A synopsis is a brief outline of a larger whole, generally given in order. John stands alone as a more interpretive work, still telling the story but with the broader purpose of establishing for readers the lordship of Christ.

What can we know about these four books and how they came to be the climactic content of our Bible? Scholars pore over every page and every phrase of them constantly and have done so for the last two centuries. While there are varying views and occasional disagreements, the basic picture that has emerged is as follows.

MARK'S FIRST SKETCH

For centuries, Mark's gospel was the least read and studied of the four—a fact that's been turned upside down during the last century.

On its face, there seemed to be nothing particularly special about Mark's book. Many felt it came across as a rough condensation of Matthew's gospel, which was by far the most popular. Matthew was lengthier, had more teachings—had more of everything, really—and those in the early church believed Matthew was written first.

Mark's gospel was the least elegantly composed of the four. It lacked key parables and great moments that could be found elsewhere. Surely Mark had simply copied the *superior* gospels. His book is abrupt and to the point.

But the key word in Mark's gospel is *immediately*. Jesus is baptized and goes immediately into the desert. The leprosy immediately leaves a man Jesus heals. There's an urgency to this gospel that points toward a resurrection all the way through but tells us very little once it has occurred.

There's very little extended teaching in Mark compared to the sermons in Matthew and Luke. The tense shifts between past and present, as it often does when we tell stories: *"And immediately the spirit driveth him into the wilderness"* (Mark 1:12 kjv). Modern translations often convert these verses to past tense for the sake of consistency, but it deprives us of that urgency. The emphasis is on action, with strong words and powerful emotions depicted; people are often *amazed*.

There are often observed details that point to eyewitness testimony, like the names of briefly sketched characters such as Bartimaeus, and the precise portion of a fishing boat where Jesus lays His head. Mark himself, we know, was no eyewitness, nor was he a fisherman, but he seems to have gotten his details from someone in the know.

Mark also uses technical Latin terminology and measures time as the Romans do, while explaining Jewish traditions to his audience. This lends credence to the tradition that Mark wrote for a Roman audience that would have struggled to identify with a crucified Savior, particularly since the Romans were the instigators of this execution.

Yet in Mark, Jesus is always pointing forward toward Jerusalem and the death that awaits Him there. Tradition also suggests that Peter himself faced the same kind of death, this time in Rome under the tyrannical emperor Nero.

Many have noticed that Peter's speech to the Roman centurion Cornelius in Acts 10:36–43 is a tight outline of Mark's gospel, beginning with the idea that Jesus *is Lord of all*" (Mark's theme), mentioning the ministry of John the Baptist, then the healings and teachings of Jesus, the trial, crucifixion, and resurrection. It's tempting to draw a line between Peter's testimony in Acts and what may be his testimony to Mark years later. Even so, if Mark used the testimony of Peter, it's also likely he drew upon that library of oral stories from the early years of church history. Many of the incidents and teachings in Mark bear the pattern of the storyteller, along with their indications of eyewitness testimony.

These are all finer points, easy to miss. In general, Mark was the favorite gospel of very few, and little study was done on it. Yet early in the twentieth century, the tide turned. Only when one compared Mark with Matthew and Luke did it become evident that earlier scholars had it backward. Mark came first, with Matthew and Luke incorporating Mark's account into their own. Matthew uses almost all of Mark in his own gospel, while Luke uses a great deal of it, and the sequencing is very similar. Both of these had access to Mark's gospel and adapted its writing, adding in some new material.

But that new material raises another problem. Matthew and Luke share a good bit of common material that isn't found in Mark— and a great deal of it seems to be sayings and parables. The best explanation for this is that they not only had access to Mark, but also to a collection of sayings that perhaps Mark didn't have. It could have been a written collection or simply an oral one; no manuscript has ever emerged to back up this theory, so some believe the *sayings gospel* never existed.

But the consensus remains that Matthew and Luke used both Mark and a collection of sayings and parables that are found in similar order in both gospels. Finally, on top of all this, we find a bit of only-in-Matthew and only-in-Luke material. For example, the beloved parables of the prodigal son and the good Samaritan are found only in Luke, while Peter's ill-fated attempt to walk on water is recorded only in Matthew.

Mark takes on added fascination when we begin to see it as *the first rough draft of history*, in the phrase of contemporary journalism. Its very roughness, immediacy, and lack of polish provide its luster. In fact, it's Mark who gives us the word *gospel*, meaning "good news":

> *The beginning of the gospel of Jesus Christ, the Son of God.*
>
> (Mark 1:1)

Mark is now studied far more closely than it once was, but the later gospels aren't ignored because they add features and perspectives essential to the Christian faith.

KING AND CAREGIVER

There are various theories as to which gospel came first, Matthew or Luke. For that matter, not everyone even agrees that Mark was the first written gospel.

One landmark event that appears nowhere in any of the Gospels is the destruction of the Second Temple by the Romans. Just about the time Mark was being written—when it's thought that both Peter and Paul were executed in Rome—a Jewish revolt began in Jerusalem. The date of AD 64 is often suggested for the martyrdom of the two apostles; Mark may have been written within five years after that. And in 70, the Roman army moved in and leveled Herod's Temple, which has never been rebuilt. (Only the Western Wall remains as a sacred reminder of what once was.) This was an incredibly traumatic event for all of Judea, and it inspired another great outflow of Jewish people into the Mediterranean world—an outflow, one could argue, that God used to send Jewish Christians out into the world to spread the blossoming faith.

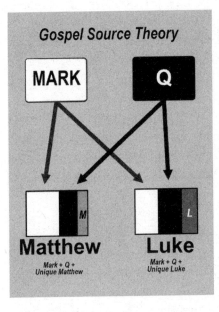

Gospel Source Theory

MARK

Q

M

Matthew
Mark + Q +
Unique Matthew

L

Luke
Mark + Q +
Unique Luke

Mark may have been written just before this event, perhaps about AD 69, and Matthew and Luke several years later. But there's no direct reference to the destruction of the temple. As a matter of fact, much attention is given to temple behavior and culture, all of which would be irrelevant post-destruction.

Still, Matthew and Luke follow Mark's lead and stay within their time frame—circa AD 30, the time of Jesus. They make extensive use of Mark, but generally shape his text for their own particular emphases. Matthew is concerned with showing how these actions of Jesus fulfilled the Hebrew prophecies. Luke wants to make the life, death, and resurrection of Jesus comprehensible for a Greek audience.

But both of them have access to a *sayings* collection of some type, whether written or simply familiar to them. Many scholars believe that both are mixing sections of this collection into Mark's narrative and their other materials.[12] This material of sayings is known to scholars as "Q," short for *quelle*, a German term for "source." The Beatitudes are part of Q. So is the Golden Rule. The Lord's Prayer, the parable of the lost sheep, and *"Judge not, that ye be not judged"* (Matthew 7:1 KJV) are quotations we find in that collection; therefore, we see them in Matthew and Luke but not in Mark.

Finally, there are also portions of these two gospels that are completely unique to their books. The unique Matthew material is

---

12. Paul J. Achtemeier, *Harper's Bible Dictionary*, Harper & Row and Society of Biblical Literature (San Francisco: Harper & Row, 1985), 1009.

known as "M," while the Luke material is "L." This chart shows the composition of Matthew and Luke, according to this theory, and the approximate ratios of each element they used. Luke uses a bit less of Mark (50 percent to Matthew's 90 percent) but has more unique material.

This isn't to say that the Mark and Q materials were simply dropped into these gospels, and that only a small amount reflects the actual Matthew or Luke. Both gospels skillfully organized the materials to reflect their own perspectives in depicting Jesus and His actions.

For example, Matthew was intended for a Jewish audience—although it was apparently written in Greek, despite Papias's belief that it was first written in Hebrew. Most likely, Matthew's audience was made up of people of Jewish heritage who were living in other countries. He quotes the Hebrew Scriptures sixty times, very often following an action by Jesus, and introduced by a phrase referring to the fulfillment of prophecy. (See, for example, Matthew 4:14.) The Hebrew sources are generally the Prophets or the Psalms. Matthew wants his audience to understand in great detail how Jesus carried out every prophecy that had been offered about the coming Messiah. His portrait of Jesus is that of the eternal King, the anointed deliverer who was foretold in many details by the Law and the Prophets.

Matthew also features the preaching of Jesus. The carefully organized gospel uses five teaching sections, including three chapters given to the Sermon on the Mount. It's sprinkled with parables and familiar miracle stories.

If Matthew sees Jesus as King, Luke underlines the love and compassion in Jesus the Caregiver. Luke, described by Paul as a physician and a personal friend, writes movingly about human emotions, as in his two key parables, the prodigal son and the good Samaritan. Luke is also unique in that his book is the first installment of a two-volume work, the sequel being the Acts of the Apostles, which succeeds the gospel. Luke and Acts were written for an audience of one: an apparent patron named Theophilus, whom Luke names at the openings of both books.

Luke observes and includes followers of Jesus other than the Twelve, including the women who were close friends of Jesus, faithful enough to follow Him to the cross and the tomb, as the eleven remaining apostles remained in hiding. In both Luke and Acts, the author spotlights the work of the Holy Spirit. And finally, Luke is a supreme historian. For many years, skeptics have sought to undermine the physician's accuracy in time and place, but he's remarkably precise in his details. Luke tells us from the beginning that he has read other gospels, handed down by the eyewitnesses, and that he set out to investigate the facts and confirm this story.

It seemed good to me also, having had perfect understanding of all things from the very first, to write to you an orderly account, most excellent Theophilus, that you may know the certainty of those things in which you were instructed. (Luke 1:3–4)

Luke fills in the gaps, sharing some of what has already been written and adding material from his own investigation. Where Matthew has told us the birth story of Jesus from the perspective of Joseph, Luke tells us Mary's story. And after the resurrection, only Luke offers us the story of the two travelers on the road to Emmaus who encounter the risen Christ.

If Mark has given us the first rough sketch of the coming of the Son of God, Matthew and Luke have gone deeper into the facts and added deeper dimensions to the portrait.

THE BELOVED DISCIPLE

John's gospel stands alone. The opposite of a rough sketch, it's a literary masterwork. Yet John makes little if any use of Q (if there was a Q), or material from the other gospels. By this time, there would be little reason for another rehash of the same material. John's gospel was almost certainly written at a late date, though still in the first century, and while we meet the very same Jesus, with His miracles, teaching, crucifixion, and resurrection, John gives us a number of stories and scenes that haven't been covered elsewhere. For example, there's Nicodemus visiting Jesus by night to learn about being born again, Jesus speaking to His disciples at great length in the upper room, and the famous encounter with the Samaritan woman at the well.

The other three gospels emphasize parables, ethical teaching, and the coming of the kingdom of God, through short sayings. In John, we have fully developed stories with longer explanations from Jesus. John uses exactly seven miracles, which he refers to as "signs," because their importance is in their meaning—what they tell us about Jesus. He uses seven "*I am*" statements from Jesus, which proceed from the central "*I AM*" identity of God, as given to Moses in Exodus 3:14. Jesus says, "*I am the bread of life,*" "*I am the light of the world,*" and "*I am the good shepherd*" (John 6:35, 8:12, and 10:11, respectively).

John is very explicit about his reason for writing a new gospel:

> *But these are written that you may believe that Jesus is the Christ, the Son of God, and that believing you may have life in His name.*   .   (John 20:31)

Throughout John's gospel, we understand that Jesus is a Man of flesh and blood, yet simultaneously the eternal Son of God. As John has told us in the first chapter, "*the Word became flesh and dwelt among us*" (John 1:14). Whereas the first three gospels are reports of the life and teachings of Jesus, John is an interpretation, and he uses every sign, every statement, and every human encounter to demonstrate the divinity and humanity of Christ.

Yet has anything changed? Mark announces, "*The beginning of the gospel of Jesus Christ, the Son of God*" (Mark 1:1). This is a consistent and unchanging theme throughout the four books. For all the comparisons and contrasts of these gospels, what is remarkable is that the portrait that emerges of Jesus is highly consistent. He may speak in short parables here and lengthy discourses there, but He is fully recognizable as the one and only Jesus of Nazareth, the peasant teacher who traveled from town to town over a short period, never held an office or any wealth, and never wrote any Scriptures Himself. He was a Man condemned and rejected by nearly everyone except a handful of followers, and yet it was this same Man's message that ultimately toppled the Roman Empire that crucified Him. In time, His message spread across every populated continent.

These four gospels are our windows into the most significant life ever lived. We know nothing about the early years of the manuscripts, other than the fact that they were obviously copied, shared, and taken abroad in their Greek language and on Roman roads. By the time the first century drew to a close, all of the books of our New Testament—letters, the Gospels, and Acts—were in circulation; from them, people began to piece together a picture of the new life of God's kingdom. What was the relationship between Jesus and God? What about the Holy Spirit? How should churches work? What was this idea of a triune God, clearly implicit in so many passages of the books but never explicitly detailed?

Jesus, Paul, and the others had provided enough material to build a worldwide movement, and that's what began to happen in the succeeding generations of Christianity. Not that there weren't problems to sort out. One of these was the growing library of literature associated with the faith. How much of it was legitimate? How much of it was worthless?

The Apostolic Fathers began working toward a consensus.

7

FAITH OF THE FATHERS

It's tempting to imagine the following scene, of which we have no actual evidence: Luke, the beloved physician, completes his two-part masterwork, telling the stories of Jesus and the church that took up His mission. Both Luke and Acts are now in the hands of patron Theophilus, so Luke turns to another project. Acts ends with Paul, still in Roman custody, freely preaching the gospel in AD 62. For reasons of his own, Luke has chosen not to write about the execution of Paul, perhaps two years later. It's possible he had no information on what happened, or even that he wrote before the beheading. We simply can't know why his account ends when it does.

Still, perhaps at this point, Luke pauses to reflect upon all of the young churches discussed in Acts and realizes the time has come to gather the writings of Paul. Churches are reading and studying them, and there's a need to have one consolidated edition of Paul's work.

Could Luke have been just the man for that job? There's no evidence of that, but he is mentioned in the letters and turns up at times in Acts, when suddenly, during parts of the journeys, Luke begins to speak of "we" instead of "they" or "he." Luke traveled with Paul and would have known and cared about these congregations.

Whether it was Luke or someone else, the writings of Paul were most assuredly gathered together early on. One of the final books of the New Testament, 2 Peter, mentions Paul's letters as a group, with the comment *"in which are some things hard to understand"* (3:16). Many people have agreed with that sentiment.

Difficult or not, it's clear that Paul's letters would have been collected by church leaders. Paul encouraged his recipients to share his letters with each other, and this would have created the pattern for a *complete works* edition. Paul also seems to have written encyclical letters that were created not just for one church but for a group of them in one region. So while Paul couldn't have imagined readers would still be perusing his work twenty centuries later, he did seem to realize his writing had lasting value, and that churches would preserve them for future reference.

Here's another point to consider: when Paul's work is compared to *"the rest of the Scriptures"* in the same verse in 2 Peter, we have a very early suggestion that already, Paul's work was being grouped with inspired writings, probably those of our Old Testament.

This was the moment when the great transition was being made from unwieldy scrolls to codex—bound stacks of vellum, papyrus, or other materials. Some believe the popularity of New Testament materials and the need to combine them expedited the process of moving to a more convenient reading medium. Yet the reverse is probably also true: that the invention of a new reading medium helped to popularize the combined study of emerging books of the Christian faith.

Either way, it simply made sense to bring together Paul's letters, most of which are relatively short. This was being done early in the second century or perhaps earlier. There also seems to have been a central copy from which others were made because the surviving editions of Paul's collection are very similar in the locations of errors or the lack thereof.

It's important to note that there were variations in what was included in the Paul collections. The later books, 1 and 2 Timothy and Titus (the Pastoral Epistles) were often excluded, yet Hebrews was included. It was often mistaken for the work of Paul, though most modern scholars believe it bears the stamp of completely different authorship.

Once the most popular gospels—Matthew, Mark, Luke, and John—were in circulation, they too would have become prime candidates for combination. Justin Martyr gives us our first known references to the reading of the gospel writings. He was born in AD 100 and was executed with friends and family for refusing to worship the emperor in 165. Despite his death, his name is *not* the source of the word *martyrdom*, as the root actually means "witness." Justin was an important writer during his period, describing early Christian worship and, in particular, the existence of "the apostles' memoirs" that were read in churches. At times, he calls these "gospels," perhaps being the first to do so.

We know that his disciple Tatian was involved even more closely with the four books detailing the life, death, and resurrection of Jesus. Tatian created the first composite gospel—not simply bringing them together but intermingling them. Like many who came after him, he wondered why one "super gospel" couldn't be compiled. This, of course, ignores the styles and nuances that make each of the four books a work worthy to stand on its own. But that's more a judgment of modern scholarship.

Tatian created what was called the *Diatessaron*, meaning "harmony of four." John's gospel provided his skeleton, to which he added the bones of the other three. He began with John 1:1–5, then inserted Luke's introduction of John the Baptist. Not surprisingly, this work proved to be immediately popular as a comprehensive biography of Jesus, and it was in print for several centuries.

But the true significance of the *Diatessaron* was as much about what Tatian didn't include as what he did. The vast majority of the book—everything but a couple of stray references—comes from Matthew, Mark, Luke, and John. This was well within the second century, and it's clear that with all of the competing gospel accounts, some of which we'll discuss in a later chapter, the early Christians had already settled on the four Gospels that mattered, the four still in use.

The next step was obvious. Once there were two collections—a gospel group and a Pauline group—it made sense to combine the two into one authoritative collection of Christian Scripture. Again, the revered medium of the scroll would have been awkward for such a large collection of writings, since it constantly would have to be rolled and unrolled. The binding of individual pages, offered by the codex, was vastly superior and allowed for referencing and cross-referencing in a more efficient manner.

F. F. Bruce, in his *The Canon of Scripture*,[13] points out that at this point, the book of Acts offered the perfect bridge between the Gospels and Paul's letters. Acts continued the story of Luke, introduced Paul and detailed his travels, and therefore it also introduced the churches to whom Paul wrote. Acts still functions that way in modern Bibles, beginning with the disciples we know and then, quite dramatically, turning its focus on the man passionate about taking the gospel to the gentile world.

The majority of our New Testament had thus been assembled. What remained were Hebrews (sometimes included with Paul), the shorter letters, and Revelation. In time, these made their way into the preferred set, though often with controversy.

Through the judgment of the church and the new technology of codices, a diverse assortment of writings became a well-established collection for the ages. But who were the leaders who navigated through these impactful decisions?

We call them the Apostolic Fathers.

THE SECOND GENERATION

As we read the Gospels, we notice the flashes of panic expressed by the disciples when Jesus speaks of leaving, specifically when He speaks of His upcoming crucifixion. They have followed Him for perhaps three years, and they've come to depend upon His judgment, His guidance, and His agenda; they depend on Him for every need that arose. When He sent them out by twos, it had to be frightening—but they trusted Him. (See Mark 6:7.) When He set His face toward Jerusalem, they understood what could and probably would

13. F. F. Bruce, *The Canon of Scripture* (Downers Grove, IL: InterVarsity Press, 1988).

happen. But the time came when the torch had to pass to a new generation. The key, of course, was for God to send His Holy Spirit. The Spirit provided courage, comfort, wisdom, and power.

Yet the next generation of followers, of everyday Christians, also became dependent upon their leaders—the disciples. They, too, must have been anxious about losing those men and women who had actually known Jesus. It's simply human nature that we look to others more experienced than ourselves, and we become apprehensive when it comes time to step out of the comfort zone. But that time does come. The apostles, plus the larger community of leaders they'd taken on—James, Matthias, Paul, Barnabas, and many others—began to vanish, either from martyrdom or simply natural causes. The "greatest generation" of Christianity was leaving the scene, and it was time for others to step up.

They always do. It's been said that the church is always one generation from extinction, but that fatal generation has never come yet. Those who replaced the apostles are known today as the Apostolic Fathers. They were *apostolic* because they had known and served Jesus's apostles personally, and that afforded them much of the same authority. They were considered to be the church's *fathers* because for many generations afterward, Christians looked to their example and their writings for guidance, as children look to parents.

These new leaders faced the challenges of a larger, more established church. They encountered more doctrinal confusion and controversy, and there was even more persecution than the apostles had faced because the church was becoming more of an empire-wide headache to the Romans.

The Apostolic Fathers are also known as the Ante-Nicene Fathers because of the Council of Nicaea in AD 325, which constituted a huge milestone in Christian history. It brought together a far-flung gathering of Christians from across the empire for the first time, it placed a fine point on the issue of Christ's identity, and it created the Nicene Creed, the first comprehensive statement of faith.

But all of this was far in the future when the second generation of believers began to take leadership. Here are three of the best-known men from that group:

CLEMENT OF ROME

Clement of Rome is often the first mentioned of these leaders. He is thought to be the same Clement mentioned by Paul as a leader of the church in Philippi. (See Philippians 4:3.) Given that he is praised in a letter by Paul that most of the churches probably read, he ultimately became leader of the important congregation in the capital of the Roman Empire.

Clement is chiefly remembered for writing a letter to the Corinthian church, just as Paul had. As usual, that church was roiled by controversy; history says the church did little else but argue. Clement counseled the congregation to respect the authority of the presbyters of that church because they'd been appointed by the apostles. The First Epistle of Clement to the church at Corinth was often read in other churches, along with the work of Paul and the other apostles. It helped to create the firm tradition of apostolic authority among church leaders. Clement's letter was a strong candidate for acceptance into the biblical canon, but in the long run, it was left behind.

Clement was thought to be the second or third bishop of Rome, and therefore became a popular figure in legends and later stories, just as Peter, Paul, and the others did. There was even a second but apocryphal letter credited to him, probably a forgery. Clement was said to have been banished from Rome by the emperor Trajan, and later martyred by being tied to an anchor that was thrown from a ship into the Black Sea.

IGNATIUS OF ANTIOCH

Ignatius of Antioch is traditionally remembered as a disciple of John, the "beloved disciple." (See John 13:23.) We know almost nothing about his life, though a later tradition claimed Ignatius was one of the children Jesus took into His arms and blessed.[14] We recall from Acts that Antioch was the first city in which followers of Jesus were known as Christians; it was one of the earliest locations of a Christian church beyond Jerusalem.

Sometime around 110, Ignatius was arrested in Antioch by a delegation of ten soldiers, who took him to Rome for execution. No one is certain why these special arrangements were followed by Rome, given that in most known cases, prisoners were executed without fanfare in their local environments.

On the journey, Ignatius penned seven letters to churches and individuals, all of which survived—though some people, including John Calvin of Geneva during the Reformation, didn't believe them to be authentic. Still, these letters were widely read and popular. Ignatius was the first to use the word *catholic*, meaning "universal," as an adjective for the church (not as a branch of Christianity, as it would be considered today). Yet he promoted only local power for bishops, not a centralized authority.

The letters of Ignatius had much to say about the nature of Christ and about church life. He was a powerful advocate of promoting the full divinity *and* full humanity of Christ and loyalty to local bishops. He called Holy Communion a "medicine of immortality." Ignatius expressed an eagerness to have his body glorified through martyrdom in the Roman arena, in being torn apart by wild animals. This seems strange to modern readers, but joyful martyrdom was a commonly stated attitude at the time, one that helped to give courage to ordinary Christians who might face persecution.

POLYCARP

Polycarp was known to be a disciple of the apostle John in Asia Minor, where John traveled after the ascension of Jesus. He was the bishop of Smyrna, now known as Izmir. His surviving letter is addressed to the Philippian church. In 155, his servants tried to

---

14. "Martyrdom of Ignatius of Antioch," Early Church History, accessed July 14, 2023, earlychurchhistory.org/martyrs/martyrdom-of-ignatius-of-antioch.

hide him from those seeking to arrest him, but Polycarp said, "God's will be done" and presented himself freely to his captors. Tradition tells us he was calm and kind to the soldiers, offering them food and drink; he only requested one final hour for prayer. Upon hearing his prayer, the soldiers were moved to shame, though they still carried out their task.

Polycarp was taken to the proconsul and faced death by burning. He was given several chances to recant, to curse Christ, or to even simply praise the emperor. But Polycarp professed his sole faith and allegiance to Christ and would not bow before any ruler. He was burned alive in the presence of a crowd and spent his final moments thanking God for the opportunity to taste from the cup of martyrs. His followers wrote a long account of his death and sent it to all the churches so that they might draw strength from his courage. The account was popular to many generations of hearers. This was the first written account of martyrdom and launched a whole genre of heroic accounts.

By his own reckoning at the execution, Polycarp was eighty-six years old when he died, one of the last of those who had known an apostle. If Polycarp died around AD 155 and lived for at least eighty-six years (as *Martyrdom of Polycarp* indicates), then he would have been born sometime around or before AD 69. This date establishes the possibility that Polycarp had contact with one or more of the apostles; this could even be the case with the later date for Polycarp's death.[15]

In his letter to the Philippians, Polycarp wrote a great deal about faith, love, and purity, with instructional sections for widows, deacons, wives, young men, virgins, and elders. He had a great concern against heresy, though apparently no particular heresy. Like many writers of this time, he peppered his prose with references taken from Paul and other New Testament writings. This showed that as soon as the early second century, the New Testament canonical books were already well-known and commonly used.

---

15. Alexander H. Pierce, "Polycarp," in *The Lexham Bible Dictionary*, ed. John D. Barry et al. (Bellingham, WA: Lexham Press, 2016).

In general, the generation of Apostolic Fathers used their writings, leadership, and frequently their deaths to edify and encourage believers during the rapid growth years of the church. Their familiarity with and use of our New Testament books went a long way toward granting them the acceptance and authority that finally made them canonical.

THE SECOND SHELF

When we discuss extrabiblical literature of the early church, most people think immediately of the apocryphal works such as the Gospel of Thomas. But it's important to remember that there were also many letters and works written, such as those by Clement, Ignatius, and Polycarp, as well as many others that are included in the library of the Apostolic Fathers. Some of these were considered part of the canon at various times. A number of titles were well-known and quoted occasionally, while others were obscure and unearthed relatively recently. Many were condemned and discarded quickly.

A great many of the apocryphal pieces have faded into the dust of antiquity, existing in mentions and occasional quotations, but not in full copies. This includes the works of Papias, the companion of Polycarp, who mentioned meeting the last surviving disciples and being given information about the writing of the Gospels. Far more was written than has been preserved. Yet there are thousands of manuscripts from New Testament writings. We can make some assessment of value to the early church by what was copied frequently enough to survive in multiple manuscripts. Even so, scholars yearn for a new discovery of some lost work of Polycarp or Clement.

All of the standard works—those that are carried in the library of the Apostolic Fathers—are in print and also readable on the Internet. We can think of them as the "second shelf" of early Christianity, the works not considered as part of the eternal Word of God, but still useful and recommended. This shelf would certainly include the letter of Clement to the Corinthians. Polycarp's writing, the letters of Ignatius, and letters by Diognetus and Barnabas would also be essential additions. We'd also find the following two works that are still popular today:

THE DIDACHE

The Didache (pronounced "Did-ah-KAY") is also known as "Teachings of the Twelve." The title shares a root word with our *didactic*, meaning teaching or instruction. This book was first written either in Egypt or Syria, and it's a very early work, possibly from late in the first century. The initial six chapters cover Christian ethics, with a memorable opening verse: "There are two ways, one of life and one of death, and there is a great difference between these two."[16] Next, the Didache takes up the sacraments, fasting, church government, and then the return of Christ and the end times.

Like most early Christian documents, the Didache quotes a great number of Old Testament verses. But many allusions and parallels to Matthew's gospel have also been found, so that it's possible a disciple of Matthew, or at least someone highly familiar with his gospel, is the author. As such an early book, the Didache is valuable for its evidence of Christian life when there was still a close connection to Judaism. This work was known through the ages, but a copy was found only as recently as 1873.

This book was also included in some early versions of the New Testament canon. However, its authorship and origins were too dubious, and while the book continued to be used in the early years, it fell from consideration as true Scripture.

THE SHEPHERD OF HERMAS

The Shepherd of Hermas was also written early, roughly during the same period as the Didache or perhaps a few years later. It may actually be a composite of two works from different periods. Hermas himself seems to have been a Jewish slave freed by Rhoda, the Roman woman who owned him. He rose in wealth and prominence, married,

---

16. Didache 1:1

but lost everything during a time of persecution. His own children disowned him, though all of them completed acts of penance later. The book is dominated by five visions that are offered as revelations from heaven. A woman from heaven brings the first four visions. The next vision comes from an angel of repentance, appearing as a shepherd and accounting for the title.

There's much material about the end times and a period of tribulation. A series of mandates and similitudes offer guidance in honoring Christ through these times. The claims of divine inspiration were taken seriously by some in the early church, who favored this book for inclusion in the New Testament for a time.

An important feature of The Shepherd is the idea of "second repentance." In the early days of Christianity, many people delayed their baptism as long as possible in order to cover more sins. There was already a misperception rampant that sins were actually forgiven in baptism rather than the act simply demonstrating or symbolizing their forgiveness. Some therefore worried over being condemned for a sin that came after baptism. The Shepherd offered the idea of another chance at repentance and forgiveness, even for those who had been through the waters. Such were issues with which the church would struggle throughout the Middle Ages.

FROM APOSTLES TO APOCRYPHALS

It's important to understand the strong dividing line between these works, most of which were accepted at least to some extent, and the much less genuine works that make up the New Testament Apocrypha—though that dividing line isn't always easy to ascertain. It should also be remembered that the glut of writings from the post-apostolic period were never generally accepted by the church at large, whereas the Old Testament Apocrypha—books such as the Maccabees, Tobit, and Judith—were actively used by the early Christians.

In the period since the intertestamental days, writing and its circulation had grown much more efficient and widespread. Common language and viable roads made culture more sharable. So while there were relatively few notable books written in the century or two before Christ, there were great numbers of them written afterward. Most of them, frankly, have not survived.

The problem was an inability for ordinary Christians and even their leaders to discern the difference between legitimate writings of the apostles and the many imitations and fakeries that were being passed around. *Pseudepigraphy* is the name for literature that is falsely attributed to a famous person, and this happened quite often with biblical personalities. For various reasons—including an effort to harm the reputation of a movement or rival—false documents were signed with forged names.

By the early second century, the gospels of Matthew, Mark, Luke, and John were quite well known and well read in congregations. But there was also a Gospel of Thomas, a Gospel of Peter, and even a Gospel of Nicodemus—none of them actually written by their stated authors. The authentic gospels, of course, were actually unsigned but associated with the given writers.

Many of the apocryphal writings have some similarities to the genuine gospels because they liberally stole from those works and imitated them. Nearly every disciple seemed to have his personal book of "Acts," such as the Acts of Peter or the Acts of Andrew. It was also possible to read an Acts of Pilate.

How about epistles? One could read Third Corinthians or Paul's epistle to Seneca the Younger. Apocalypses, in the style of Revelation, were also in vogue and available as the supposed work of various famous Christians. "Secret Gospels" promised hidden information that Jesus didn't share with just anybody. Nearly all of these books, of course, were written many decades—sometimes a century or more—after those that were in the process of becoming canonized as our New Testament.

In short, there was inspired material in circulation, but also no shortage of malicious fakery. Some things never change.

At various times, particularly in recent years, certain critics have stepped forward to claim these lesser-known gospels and epistles were wronged when church leaders pushed them aside. Some form of political struggle or backroom conspiracy is blamed; supposedly, a certain set of books is said to have won out over an equally qualified set that was left to fade into obscurity. The canonization process is covered in a later chapter, but for now, it's worth remembering that canonization was something our New Testament books *earned* over a lengthy period of time, not as a result of some council or happenstance. As early as the end of the first century, Matthew, Mark, Luke, and John were the gospels in use.

QUESTIONABLE GOSPELS

As for the questionable gospels in circulation, two vivid examples will suffice:

THE INFANCY GOSPEL OF THOMAS

For those who crave stories of Jesus's childhood, the Infancy Gospel of Thomas supposedly fills in some of the blanks. According to this gospel, at the age of five, Jesus plays beside a creek with other children, making clay from the water. He forms a few sparrows from the clay, then brings them to life so they can fly away. Another child approaches Jesus from behind and begins splashing water with a stick. Angry at the child's treatment of harmless water, Jesus turns around and curses him to wither up like a tree that will never bear leaves. The child indeed withers.

THE GOSPEL OF PETER

The Gospel of Peter, finally discovered in 1886, created quite a commotion once it was read. In this vivid recounting of the tomb story, the soldiers are keeping watch as the Sabbath dawns. They see the heavens open, and two men, clothed in light, descend and approach the tomb. The stone blocking the tomb then rolls away of its own accord, and the two strangers go inside. But *three* men emerge, two supporting one who is apparently not sure on his feet. Also, there is a wooden cross walking behind them. The heads of the two brightly lit men reach to heaven, but the third man is even taller—his head surpasses the heavens. A voice from heaven speaks to the cross, and the cross answers, "Yes." Apparently the cross was also buried and resurrected.

Talking crosses notwithstanding, the era of dubious Scriptures at least demonstrates the wild popularity not only of the Jesus story, but of all the surrounding elements—the disciples, Paul, Mary, even second-generation heroes in some cases. In general, the church wasn't confused by these imitation gospels and epistles. Bishops and leaders seemed to know where to find the real thing. Even so, the issue of canonization—separating the wheat from the chaff—became more important.

It was time to finalize what we've come to call the New Testament.

8

A BATTLE OF IDEAS

During its first two centuries, Christianity was growing at a rate of 40 percent per decade, according to Rodney Stark's recent study, *The Rise of Christianity*. His research suggests there were 40,000 Christians in AD 150. By the year 200, there were 218,000, including new Swiss and Belgian churches. There were 1.7 million by 250, and Christianity had reached Paris.[17]

The unimposing, ragtag band of believers in the book of Acts outlasted the Roman Empire itself within a century of that.

In those first two centuries, Christianity was mostly found in cities, along the lines of the strategies of Paul and others in planting them. First, Paul sought places with lots of people, where there were synagogues and a Jewish audience capable of understanding the prophecies. He understood the future belonged to the rest of the world, of which Judaism was just a tiny, obscure portion. His mission was to present the gospel to non-Jews, but the starting point had to be those who worshiped the same God.

But time began to distance Christianity from its Jewish roots—roots that had served as a kind of safeguard, affixing the movement to the unique and specific Hebrew Scriptures. The person of Jesus is understood through the lens of God's Old Testament covenants. He is described by Paul as the second Adam. (See Romans 5:12–21.) He's depicted by the prophets as being from the house of David. He taught through the experiences and words of Abraham and Moses, and He was the Messiah, the deliverer of one particular belief tradition.

---

17. Philip Jenkins, "How Many Christians?", Patheos, September 22, 2017, citing Rodney Stark, *The Rise of Christianity: A Sociologist Reconsiders History* (Princeton University Press, 1996), www.patheos.com/blogs/anxiousbench/2017/09/how-many-christians.

Yet from the beginning, some set out to cut the new movement loose from its historic foundation. They wanted Jesus freed of context.

Things were coming full circle. In the beginning, as shown in Acts, Jewish believers expected gentiles to fully embrace the Mosaic law and its traditions, down to circumcision and daily diet. This, as we know, was to err in the opposite direction. Paul understood that those restrictions were no longer necessary.

But after a century, many Christians of Europe, Asia, and northern Africa weren't convinced they should worry about Jewish history and law *at all*. Wasn't Jesus for all nations and all people? Why worry about the Jewish people and their stories and traditions?

Therefore, there was a growing problem within flourishing Christianity. Its Jewish roots were in question. The movement could be victimized by its own success, by forgetting where it came from. How could the Christian faith break into so many cultures and languages, take on so many new believers, and meet the needs of all people everywhere while rooted in the Jewish faith?

MARCIONISM

A challenge to Hebrew scriptural relevance came as early as the mid-second century. Marcion, the prominent son of a bishop in Sinope, in present-day Turkey, came of age with a heightened adoration of the writings of Paul—so much so that he decided Paul was the only true apostle.

He noted Paul's passion about salvation from grace rather than the law, and thus concluded that the law was a relic of the past—and the Old Testament with it. When Marcion configured one of the first lists of a biblical canon, he created a very thin Bible that included Luke's gospel, minus the birth narrative, and ten letters of Paul. All else was discarded—not only the Old Testament but also any reference to it in the New Testament. There simply couldn't be any discussion of the Law and the Prophets or anything related to Jewish heritage, which was now deemed irrelevant.

This required some editing, even in Luke and the Pauline Epistles. Jesus was always quoting the Hebrew Scriptures, so these references had to be cut out. Luke's nativity account had to go because Marcion believed that Jesus came to earth fully formed and wouldn't have been involved in anything as untidy as human birth.

Some passages in Luke or even Paul's writings didn't measure up to Marcion's conception of Christian truth, so he rewrote some verses. He also believed the creator God of the Old Testament was a separate being from the loving God of the New. This was the clear influence of Gnosticism, which we will discuss more fully in a bit. In a nutshell, Marcion believed that the lesser God created the material world, which he felt to be flawed and evil, and the later God was a God of the Spirit.

Somehow Marcion expected to be hailed as a theological genius. He was shocked when his views were rejected on a trip to Rome. As a matter of fact, his substantial financial contribution to the church was returned to him in full, and he withdrew from fellowship with the Christian church as it stood. His movement, Marcionism, had to win converts aggressively; given the evils of the flesh, as he understood sex, everyone who followed him had to swear to celibacy, so there would be no Marcionite children. In any case, it didn't remain a problem for long because the Marcionites broke into arguing camps, and the movement faded away.

Marcion actually made a contribution to Christianity more enduring than his financial one ever could have been. He forced the church to realize it must define what was and wasn't Scripture, particularly regarding how the Hebrew materials should be handled. If Marcion made this challenge, he wouldn't be the last.

Fortunately, the consensus was that the Hebrew writings were as relevant as ever, inseparable from the Christian message and worthy to be read and discussed in worship settings. In a remarkable way, the Christian movement continued to grow at an exponential rate, moving into parts of Europe or Asia, where Hebrew culture was unfamiliar, and yet retained its spiritual and historic foundation in the world of Abraham, Moses, David, and Isaiah.

MONTANISM

Looking to history, the Hebrew Scriptures could be affirmed. But what about this side of the cross? When, if ever, did divine revelation conclude? The church now had to answer this question with the coming of Montanus, a pagan priest who converted to Christianity in a small village in the Asian portion of present-day Turkey.

Montanus was no quiet philosopher. He spoke in ecstatic utterances, tongues, and prophecy that he claimed came from God. He even insisted that he was the Paraclete—the Advocate, that is, the Holy Spirit—of whose coming Jesus had spoken in John's Gospel.

As he traveled with two women who also claimed to have special gifts, Montanus attracted a great deal of attention and followers, possibly because of the power of spectacle. His brief moment of fame came in the 170s. And for a brief period, he attracted approval from Tertullian, a well-respected leader in the early church.

But others were quick to condemn the Montanists. Their leader promoted the coming return of Christ, the New Jerusalem, strict abstinence from most forms of pleasure (asceticism), and the importance of spiritual gifts; the glaring controversies were his suggestion that God was still revealing new truth, and that he himself was a manifestation of the Spirit of God.

The church of that time had questions. Was the body of inspired Scripture complete, or could someone like Montanus claim to offer something new from heaven? Jerome, the Christian scholar writing three centuries later, summarized the chief objection to Montanism: its idea that God's revelation in Christ was incomplete, still needing the word of Montanus and the two women who accompanied him. Jerome's contention was that God had spoken once and for all time through Jesus.

Montanus was dismissed by Christian leaders as a heretic, but again, he gave the church more reason to define what was and was not divinely inspired.

GNOSTICISM

Perhaps the greatest doctrinal challenge of all was that of Gnosticism. Its great dangers were that it was so widespread, took so many forms, and seemed to infiltrate Christian thinking at every turn. Preliminary versions of the heresy were already circulating in the first century, and the letters in the New Testament make reference to the false teachers spreading them. (See, for example, Romans 16:17–18; Colossians 2:8; 1 Timothy 1:3–7; Titus 1:11.)

Gnosticism wasn't one simple, consistent movement with identifiable leaders and Scriptures. It was a body of Greek teachings based around the idea that salvation comes through knowledge (*gnosis*). The Gnostics were obsessed with the idea that this knowledge was in the form of secrets, available only to special people.

The Gnostics pointed out that Jesus, particularly early in His ministry, told certain people to be secretive about what they witnessed. (See, for example, Mark 7:36.) He also said that He spoke in parables so that only His disciples would understand. (See Matthew 13:10–11.) The Gnostics maintained that only very special people possessed this secret knowledge. The Gospel of Thomas, a *sayings* gospel that seems to be influenced by Gnosticism, begins, "These are the hidden sayings that the living Jesus spoke and Didymos Judas Thomas wrote down. And he said, 'Whoever discovers the meaning of these sayings won't taste death.'"[18]

Gnosticism presents a dualistic view of the universe, one in which evil is as powerful as good, and all material reality is evil while all spirit is good. Some kind of *divine spark* from God, becoming a lesser divinity, created the physical world. But what about Jesus taking on human flesh? Only an illusion, according to Gnostic thinkers. Jesus

18. *The Gospel of Thomas*, www.gospels.net/thomas.

was pure Spirit, they said, only creating the deceptive image of physicality. Humans themselves are divine spirits imprisoned in physical bodies, which are to be hated.

Gnosticism was a version of neither Judaism nor Christianity, having foundational differences with both. But as it paid special attention to Jesus, made certain use of the Scriptures, and shared the same cultural spaces, it had a way of slipping into churches. Gnostic writings were also in abundance, often difficult for the undiscerning to differentiate from the genuine articles.

The Apostolic Fathers had set about the task of encouraging and nurturing the young church. The next generation of leaders, during the mid- to late-second century, had the assignment of combating heresy, Gnosticism in particular. They began to write tracts and letters taking on these false teachings, and this also inspired them to use the inspired, accepted Scriptures as ammunition. Whereas the purpose of the Gospels and letters had always been to edify believers through worship readings, now they had to be used to combat error as *"the sword of the Spirit, which is the word of God"* (Ephesians 6:17).

After several of these controversies had bubbled to the surface, it became clear that even beyond the use and definition of the Scriptures, some kind of creedal system was needed, a shorthand way to inform all believers of the essentials of their faith. As things stood, Christian leaders appealed to what they called the *rule of faith* as their authority. That is, if a claim was made about some spiritual issue, the standard for evaluation was that it had to agree with basic Christian traditional ideas as set forth by the Hebrew Scriptures and the early church.

In time, the rule of faith was expressed by the Nicene Creed and the Apostles' Creed.

THE MURATORIAN LIST

The church was in the midst of determining the preferred Scriptures by sheer usage. Four gospels were unchallenged as authoritative: three Synoptics and one more interpretive biography by John. Paul's letters, along with several others, were also in usage to various degrees. There were books such as James, Jude, and 2 Peter that were considered to be less firmly part of the set; others, such as the Didache or Clement's letter, were viewed as something very close to inspired.

But there were disagreements about books such as Hebrews and Revelation. Where was it written which books could and should be used? As the new controversies inspired new arguments, counterarguments, and defenses, it became important to know the boundaries of authority.

Some began to make lists of approved books. Marcion, of course, had his list, which was short, limited, and highly conditional upon his personal deletions and additions: Luke and some of Paul. Perhaps the first legitimate list appears in a fragment from a very rare document known as the Muratorian Fragment. This ragged document was a copy of a copy, several hundred years after the list was first written. Like so many rare documents, it was found in an obscure monastery. Scholars believe it was first written at the end of the second century because it refers to a pope from the mid-second century as "recent."

While it's simply a list of New Testament books, it's important in that lists of this type aren't much in evidence from the period, and it also reflects something close to the New Testament canon as it now stands. To add extra value, the list carries commentary that gives us a glimpse of how those books were regarded by Christian leaders of the time, including a few comments on rejected books.

In truth, Matthew and Mark are not included, but this is no cause for concern because the document is torn, with its first few lines missing. The first readable item, Luke, is described as the "third gospel." It seems safe to assume, knowing the universal acceptance of the first two gospels and their usual given order, that Matthew and Mark would appear in any complete version of the document.

The Muratorian writer introduces the Gospels and Paul's epistles, describing key features of each. He mentions that John (in Revelation) has written letters to seven churches that can be read with good results by all assemblies of believers, and that Paul has also written letters to seven churches that could be used for edification. (Galatians is written to several churches.)

But then the writer mentions two letters attributed to Paul—to the Laodiceans and the Alexandrines—that are "forged in accordance with Marcion's heresy."[19] These and many other letters, we read, cannot be received into the church "since it is not fitting that poison should be mixed with honey."[20]

He then affirms Jude and two letters of John (we can't know which two of the three) and, surprisingly, the Wisdom of Solomon, a first-century book from Alexandra that we tend to group with the Old Testament Apocrypha, despite its late date.

The Apocalypse of John (Revelation) is accepted, as is the Apocalypse of Peter, a second-century apocalyptic letter. Some, he adds, will not allow the latter to be read in church.

The Shepherd of Hermas is complimented but not affirmed as Scripture; the Muratorian writer reasons that it is too recent a composition. And several other unacceptable books are mentioned.

Ultimately, we have a list, probably from the late second century, that establishes the majority of the books that would become the New Testament canon and also shows a considerable level of discernment in recognizing low-value books. This is invaluable evidence as to the standing of ancient Christian books relatively early in the movement.

AGAINST HERESIES

Meanwhile, the more learned leaders of the church continued to speak out against false teaching. The great defender of the faith during the second century was Irenaeus, who grew up listening to the

19. Bruce, *The Canon of Scripture*, 160.
20. Ibid.

preaching of Polycarp in Asia, but relocated to Lyons, France, to serve as a presbyter. Eventually, Irenaeus became bishop but found his true calling as a writer of Christian theology. *Against Heresies* is his best-known work. In this volume, he went after Marcion and Valentinus, a fellow Gnostic of the same period, arguing for a traditional and scriptural faith in continuity with the God revealed in the Old Testament.

As Irenaeus saw it, Christ had taught the apostles, who taught the church fathers who came after them, and doctrinal authority proceeded in a straight line in that fashion. The positive outcome of that reasoning comes in the conservatism of a received legacy of truth that guards against heresy coming from the outside. Tradition deserves honor and respect. For modern observers, the danger would be in overcentralizing Christian authority as opposed to considering Christ as high priest for each individual. Hundreds of years later, at the outset of the Reformation, these questions would heat up. The idea of authority through succession helped lead to arguments for a high bishop, or pope.

Irenaeus drew strongly from the Scriptures to defend his opinion. He was the first writer to list the four gospels in the context of a canon. He then listed much of the rest of the accepted apostolic writings, added the Hebrew Scriptures, and referred to all of it as "Scripture." These may seem like small details, but they present evidence of views toward the Gospels and letters early in church history.

In challenging the Gnostic idea of spirit versus physicality, Irenaeus affirmed the goodness of God's creation. Overall, he was more in tune with biblical ideas, particularly those of Paul, than most leaders of his time. He understood all of Christianity to proceed from the truth of Christ Himself. After Paul, Irenaeus can be considered the father of Christian theology.

THE AGE OF COUNCILS

Through the 200s, Christianity continued its remarkable surge. In 202, the Roman emperor, Septimius Severus, issued an edict forbidding Christian conversion. Six years later, Tertullian wrote about Christianity in England, where Roman rule and the new faith were both making inroads. In 270, the monastic movement began with Anthony of Egypt, a foreshadowing of the Middle Ages to come. The idea was to create a new kind of Christian community where there was no interference from worldly princes.

By the year 300, Christianity was moving deeper into Asia, and some estimate that 10 percent of the world's population was Christian.[21] Yet the worst of all persecutions of the church began in 303, when the Roman emperor Diocletian began enforcing local religious practices on Christian believers. He also burned any Scriptures that could be located.

Only a decade later, the emperor was Constantine, and after claiming to see a vision, he himself converted to Christianity. In 313, his Edict of Milan finally established full acceptance for those following Jesus.

Throughout the second century, various synods or councils were convened to discuss doctrines and heresies. But with empire-wide acceptance, it was now possible to hold something larger: "worldwide" (for the time) ecumenical councils. Christianity spanned three continents, so the bishops were concerned about the diverging traditions and beliefs throughout Christendom. Consensus on key issues would be important for the unity of Christianity.

Across the next 450 years, there were seven ecumenical councils, the best known coming at the beginning, in 325: the First Council of Nicaea. The city where it was held is now known as Iznik, Turkey. Significantly, Constantine himself invited 1,800 bishops, only two decades after the horrendous persecution under his predecessor Diocletian.

The greatest accomplishment of the Council of Nicaea was its rulings on the nature of Christ. The heresy of the day was Arianism. Arius claimed that Jesus Christ was created by the Father; since He

---

21. Rodney Stark, *The Rise of Christianity* (San Francisco: Harper, 1997), 7.

was a "begotten" Son, He was born. The council ruled that Jesus is coeternal with the Father, uncreated, "of the same essence" as the Father (*homo-ousias*), and fully divine. Even today, these are considered foundational, orthodox doctrines throughout the Christian faith.

These rulings were based on careful study of the Gospels and the letters of the apostles. The council also began the first versions of what became the Nicene Creed, also known as the Niceno-Constantinopolitan Creed. This statement of faith was designed to help believers summarize the key elements of Christian doctrine, including the truth of one God, the three persons of the Trinity, the virgin birth of Jesus, His crucifixion and resurrection, His return in glory, and the resurrection of the dead.

The council did not establish a biblical canon. There's actually no mention of Scripture in the Nicene Creed other than "in accordance with the Scriptures," a reference to Old Testament prophecy. The issue was considered largely resolved by that time. No ecumenical or other type of council ever established a ruling on the canon. Through the ages, there has been a myth that Constantine or the bishops at Nicaea gathered to promote some books as official and canonical and condemn others. This idea was first stated seven centuries later in a Greek manuscript that spun the tall tale of the bishops placing all of the various books beside a table and praying for God to place the ones He approved on the table while casting the rest on the floor. It happened just that way, miraculously, according to this one belated account, and that's how we have our New Testament.

In the twentieth century, Dan Brown's thriller novel *The Da Vinci Code* made the appalling claim that Constantine actively suppressed eighty gospels while promoting the only four that showed Jesus as being divine. He claimed that the true, earlier gospels that were suppressed showed that Jesus was simply a man. The millions of people who read the book or saw the movie sometimes assumed that even though the main characters were fictional, these claims must be based on some valid bit of history. As a result, the myth of

Constantine determining a bogus canon is alive and well, despite being in error.

The true earlier gospels—the ones we still use today—were written by earlier men who knew and walked with Jesus. An even "earlier" man, Paul of Tarsus, professed the full divinity of Christ almost immediately after the resurrection. As a matter of fact, our accepted gospels present a nuanced view of Jesus in His full humanity and His full divinity. All four are clear on both aspects of His nature. A *merely human* Jesus isn't anywhere to be found in ancient literature.

These issues continued to be debated through ecumenical councils to come. The Scriptures enshrine these concepts, but their finer points are elusive. For example, the Trinity—God in three persons—isn't explicitly laid out in a detailed way, yet key passages of the New Testament clearly assume the doctrine. For example, in several of his letters, Peter offers these words that seem to be a common salutation of his time: *"The grace of the Lord Jesus Christ, and the love of God, and the communion of the Holy Spirit be with you all"* (2 Corinthians 13:14). The nature of Christ and the reality of the Trinity are present with consistency, though they must be gathered by taking the full counsel of Scripture. This is what the early synods and councils set out to accomplish.

And as they did so, they used the most consistent and reliable sources—the twenty-seven books we call the New Testament. They used them not out of some political agenda or bias, but because truth was evident in them, and they were historically relevant. Harvard Professor Arthur Darby Nock, who was a world-class scholar on the history of religion, used this metaphor when discussing how the biblical canon came together: "The most travelled roads in Europe are the best roads; that is why they are so heavily travelled."[22]

From the earliest days onward, these twenty-seven books were recognized as the best roads to the eternal truth about Jesus Christ and the wonderful grace of God.

---

22. Bruce M. Metzger, *The Canon of the New Testament: Its Origin, Development, and Significance* (New York: Oxford University Press, 1987), 286.

9

THE LIBRARY IS CLOSED

W_e can imagine a meeting between two bishops early in the second century. The bishop of Lystra has made a journey to Iconium, no more than twenty miles away. Many years earlier, Paul and Barnabas had visited both cities on their first missionary journey. They'd faced persecution then, but the churches had ultimately taken hold and grown.

The bishop of Iconium welcomes his friend to his home; they speak of their ministries and the challenges of their cities. Then the host says, "Oh! It almost slipped my mind. I have something to show you." Taking his friend to a special, well-crafted wooden box where he stores his documents, he removes two rolls of parchment. "I have two new letters," he says. "I copied them myself on a visit to Antioch, and I'm happy to loan you pen and parchment to make your own copies."

The bishop of Lystra is immediately interested. "But are they real?" he asks. "I see more and more letters and writings floating about, and sometimes it's difficult to tell whether they're real or imitation. Most of them these days seem to be worthless."

"This is one reason I'd like you to copy them, my friend—to help me ascertain that very thing. Like you, I will not read them in our worship unless I feel confident the Spirit of God truly speaks to us through them."

Perhaps this type of scene occurred fairly regularly in the early days of the church. If you were a part of this new and exciting movement, your written Scriptures would be precious, essential—but you would always wish there were more. It would be natural to hope that someone would find another gospel written by a disciple that, for whatever reason, had just come to light. Or perhaps a letter of Paul that hadn't previously been made public.

There were people who enjoyed falsifying the works of Christian heroes. But every now and then, there was something that might actually be interesting, though not qualifying as Scripture.

It was good to speak with other bishops and Christian leaders, particularly those who were old and wise, able to discern truth from fakery. We know churches exchanged letters that were known to be authentic so that everyone could benefit from their wisdom. Paul encourages churches to exchange letters in Colossians 4:16. But John encourages them to be careful about what they accept:

> Beloved, do not believe every spirit, but test the spirits, whether they are of God; because many false prophets have gone out into the world. By this you know the Spirit of God: Every spirit that confesses that Jesus Christ has come in the flesh is of God.
>
> (1 John 4:1–2)

We notice John's key criteria: the physicality of Jesus—"*Jesus Christ has come in the flesh.*" That standard immediately rules out any Gnostic writings. Those documents that understand that Jesus is true God and true Man are the ones that are authentic.

As time went on, the task of *testing the spirits* grew easier. If the thought of a new gospel seemed too good to be true, it invariably was. The four gospel writings were part of a collection every bishop had; they came in a set. The same was true of Paul's letters. There was no reason for someone to collect just one of them. Third Ephesians or a second epistle to the Romans was unlikely to turn up after a certain period of time.

Still, it was good to have an open mind, to read and study carefully, to pray on the matter, and particularly to hide the true and divine Scriptures in one's heart. The more one knew the truth of

God's kingdom and the reality of the immortal God made flesh, the more difficult it would be to be fooled.

Fairly early, the majority of the authoritative Christian collection was firm and well-established. There was almost never any real doubt over the Gospels, Acts, or the letters of Paul. Only a few books—Hebrews, Revelation, 2 Peter, and Jude, for example—seemed to invite disagreement.

When it came down to making a case for why a book should or shouldn't be included, the Apostolic Fathers had certain criteria that they considered.

MEETING THE CREDENTIALS

The early church fathers, who followed the first generation of eyewitnesses and participants in the ministry of Jesus, used several criteria in deciding whether to assign authority to a writing. This *criteria of canonicity* wasn't a formal system, but more a pattern of questions we derive from studying their writings over the course of their leadership. They often discussed these books, and when they did, they would clarify their objections to a book in question.

The issue for that generation was: Can this work be read in worship? The Apostolic Fathers were not cavalier about church readings. They insisted on certainty that God was speaking to a new generation through the written word, in the scriptural tradition. The Hebrew canon was acceptable for worship reading. But what about newer writings?

Here are the questions they considered:

+ *Was it written by the apostles?*

The apostles were granted authority and power by Jesus. If an apostle surely wrote this work, then it should be read for all Christians to hear. As we've seen, that wasn't always a clear issue. The four gospels were all anonymous, though everyone basically agreed on who wrote what. It's also true that if a gospel or letter *was* signed, that didn't make it authentic. One had to guard against forgeries. Apostolic authorship was the most important credential, but it was important to have others to bolster their candidacy for worship reading.

* *Does it follow the rule of faith?*

That is, is this work in line with core Christian beliefs taught by Jesus and then the apostles? The *rule of faith*, an appeal to the basic, known teachings, was used in the second century for interpretation of Scripture. In time, the Nicene Creed, the Apostles' Creed, and other statements of faith became the substance of the rule of faith.

* *Is this document accepted across Christendom?*

The word used was *catholic*, meaning "universal," a statement of geography not affiliation. If churches in both Asia and Europe accepted a document or an idea, it must be orthodox—that is, acceptable practice.

* *Has it stood the test of time?*

New writings were suspicious writings. The longer a manuscript had been in existence and usage—particularly if that included the time of the apostles—the more likely it was to be trusted. It was highly unlikely a manuscript written during the previous month was going to be shared with the congregation.

* *Was it part of a collection?*

Paul's letters were gathered and kept together by the end of the first century. They weren't circulated individually but as a group. The same was true of the Gospels. In a collection, any particular document was given gravitas by its association with the other documents. At times, the *Pastoral Epistles*—1 and 2 Timothy and Titus—weren't universally accepted, but as part of the Pauline collection, they ultimately gained approval.

CLEARLY INSPIRED

It wasn't always necessary to meet all of these criteria. Some of the books that were eventually accepted into the canon failed to meet one or more of the criteria. There were also books that did not meet enough of the most essential criteria, such as the Shepherd of Hermas. The author of the Muratorian Fragment found this work worthwhile for reading material, but not for sharing in worship because it failed the *test of time*. Neither was it apostolic or accepted across Christendom.

Clearly the gospel and Pauline collections passed with flying colors. They met all the criteria. There were close calls among several later epistles, including 2 Peter, Jude, and 2 and 3 John. But in the end, canonization meant affirmation by the church that this was the inspired Word of God. Other works might be fine material, edifying spiritually, but simply not divine revelation. That was the ultimate standard: certainty of divine inspiration. When two or more gathered for worship, only the voice of God Himself should be heard.

It's a tribute to the early church that twenty-seven books made the cut, that all of these were early in time of writing, and that no others were added through politics or any other pressure. The Shepherd of Hermas and the Didache were quite popular and thought to carry worthy instruction, but that wasn't enough to place them in the category of the revealed Word of God.

This demonstrates that early on, the twenty-seven accepted books were viewed as divinely inspired. They didn't begin as reading material that took on trappings of holiness over time until they were *declared* inspired. From the beginning, only these were allowed to be read in worship, while other titles, even good ones, were disallowed.

The idea was that God had sent His Son into the world and had then inspired followers of His Son to tell the good news in writing so that future generations would have an objective, written testimony to balance the indwelling, *felt* testimony of the Holy Spirit. Only these early, inspired heralds of the kingdom were part of that work of God.

Recency became a very difficult objection to overcome. As we read the discussions from the Apostolic Fathers, we notice how frequently they cite the lateness of a book as an objection. Documents from the second century and certainly afterward ultimately never found acceptance.

The rule of faith comes up almost as often. The leaders were vigilant in guarding against any signs of Gnosticism in particular. Denial of the physical nature of Jesus or the goodness of God's physical creation quickly brought condemnation on writings or teachings.

And while we see so many books listed as apocryphal works of the time—many of them no longer available—those who haven't studied the period often assume that the early church had its hands full in evaluating this flood of literature. Yet in truth, a great many of the titles never appear in discussions among the church fathers. Even in a time of tremendous controversy and doctrinal challenge, the selection of Scripture wasn't particularly controversial.

A remarkable trove of mostly gnostic documents was found near Nag-Hammadi in Egypt, along the Nile, in 1945. Titles from the find include the Prayer of the Apostle Paul, the Secret Book of James, the Gospel of Truth, the Gospel of Philip, On the Origin of the World, Holy Book of the Great Invisible Spirit or the Gospel of the Egyptians, the Dialogue of the Savior, and the famous Gospel of Thomas (in the only known complete version), among many others. But almost none of these were discussed by the early Christian leaders. It might be that they never even saw most of these books.

It also seems that nearly all the apocryphal selections were rejected not just in key locations, but across Christendom. For example, the Shepherd of Hermas was not considered canonical among the Eastern churches while being disavowed in the West. There were regional disagreements and differences in the Christian world, but very few when it came to Scripture. The exception was that some of the Eastern churches continued to have reservations about Revelation, Hebrews, and the other writings a bit longer than the West.

There was far less controversy over canon than might be expected. The strongest reason for this was that the criteria for recognizing valid inspiration was effective.

TOGETHER FOR THE FIRST TIME

When we first learn that the canon of Scripture was set down only at the end of the fourth century, it can seem odd. What took so long? Those with little background knowledge might even think there was no real Bible until the year AD 400. Obviously, this is far from the case. If deciding which books to accept had truly been a matter of great controversy, surely it would have been taken up at the Council of Nicaea in 325. At that council, the date for celebrating Easter was considered a hot topic, but it still wasn't quite resolved.

But there was little disagreement on the topic of which writings could be read in worship and used for spiritual guidance. Churches everywhere were using the four gospels and the letters of Paul and others. Finally, however, it seemed necessary for the church to speak on the matter and establish a clear ruling. One part of the reason was technology.

The process of binding a codex into a folio had moved along so that all twenty-seven Christian books could be bound together— something that must have delighted church leaders and those fortunate enough to own a Bible and possess the ability to read it. Just as the coming of the New Testament writings expedited the development of the codex, the completion of the canon was the perfect vehicle for the new and enlarged codex that was one step closer to the modern Bible.

There had been collections at this point—one of Paul, one of the Gospels. These were thought of as units, smaller books in themselves. It's even possible to speculate that the other letters were less popular because they didn't fit so neatly into a collection, other than a miscellaneous one. There were other perceived issues, to be sure, but compared to a set of the Gospels, the Acts, and the works of Paul, the grouping of Hebrews, Revelation, and assorted short letters seemed like something of a grab bag.

But there was a philosophical change implied by binding all of the books into a whole—a master collection of Christian Scriptures that emphasized the unity of the work. It all fit together in a logical order: the life of Jesus, the activities of His followers including Paul in Acts, then Paul's letters, then the letters of others, and finally a book on the end times and the judgment of Christ, now in glory. One could easily pray and reflect on a passage from Romans, then flip quickly to the Gospels to read a passage that came to mind. And what a joy to read the Gospel of Luke and the Acts of the Apostles within one binding!

Binding, too, offers a handy metaphor for the purpose of a canon. What is a *canon* anyway? It's a group of materials to whose truth and teaching we're bound.

Not surprisingly, it comes from a Greek term *kanon*, meaning "reed." (The English word *cane*, as in sugarcane, comes from this root word.) In the ancient world, a reed could be plucked and used as a measuring rod, a standard by which to compare lengths. So *canon*, once it began to appear in church discussions, was a standard, something to measure against. Athanasius (296–373), as we'll see, was the first to apply the word *canon* to the idea of accepted Scripture.[23] His context was a statement that's grown familiar: the Shepherd of Hermas was good for reading, he opined, but did not belong in the canon.

The canon, as should be obvious by now, came together not by decree or by vote but by honoring the *well-traveled roads* of scriptural truth, to use Professor Nock's apt metaphor from the close of the previous chapter. The Gospels and the letters of Paul in particular were embraced and trusted from the beginning; there was never much doubt about any of this material. The more controversial books took a bit more discussion and the wisdom of time for making a determination.

---

23. Bruce, *The Canon of Scripture*, 77.

Hebrews, James, 2 Peter, 2 and 3 John, Jude, and Revelation were the books at issue. Of those, Hebrews is certainly a popular book today, with many beloved passages. Questions over authorship held it back from full embrace. Peter's second letter seemed too different in style from the first letter, which was well accepted. That raised flags for some. James, for some, presented conflicts with Paul's theology. In any case, James and Jude were identified as "servants" rather than apostles in their introductions. Similarly, 2 and 3 John were seldom-used letters with questions of authorship, and John, the author, claimed only to be an elder. But in time, each of these books would be seen as inspired Scripture.

Final determinations, in the form of announcements from the church, were eventually made for several reasons. Along with the desire to add inspired Christian books to the collection, the church wanted to formalize the canon when it became clear that heresy wasn't about to go out of style. More time was being spent combatting Gnosticism and the other stubborn ideas that grew out of poor representations of the Christian faith. Just to list a few, Docetism, Adoptionism, Nestorianism, Apollinarianism, Donatism, Pelagianism, and Manicheanism were all early heresies from this time period, most of them having to do with the nature of Christ or the Trinity. There needed to be a strong, well-attested set of Christian books that stood together and offered a united front in fighting off these viral eruptions of misguided theology.

A final reason for the eventual statement of a canon was that in times of persecution, which still occurred in some places, one of the first crises was the burning of literature. Christians needed to know which writings could be given up and which needed to be hidden and guarded vigilantly.

EUSEBIUS MAKES A LIST

By the time Eusebius came into prominence as the bishop of Caesarea, Christianity was approaching its three hundredth year.

Someone needed to write a history, and Eusebius eventually provided a ten-volume one called *The Church History* or *Ecclesiastical History*. He had access to a wealth of literature in Caesarea's library that is no longer in existence, so he is virtually our only source of information on many matters. Beyond his stature as the "Father of Church History," he is important to the history of the Bible for at least two reasons.

He was commissioned in 330 by the emperor Constantine to provide fifty copies of New Testament Scripture to the bishop of Constantinople. These were to be written in Greek and made available to the many new churches forming in that area. In his history, Eusebius quoted the emperor's letter:

> I have thought it expedient to instruct your Prudence to order fifty copies of the sacred Scriptures, the provision and use of which you know to be most needful for the instruction of the Church, to be written on prepared parchment in a legible manner, and in a convenient, portable form, by professional transcribers thoroughly practiced in their art.[24]

We can't be certain this commission was finally carried out, and most scholars doubt any of the fifty copies are still in existence. The importance of the request is that Eusebius and others would have had to make a judgment on which items to include in any complete collection of Scripture. As it happens, we can guess, because Eusebius covered his own thoughts and the opinions of others in his *History*.

Eusebius finds three classifications of Christian works. First, he lists the fully accepted ones: the four gospels, Acts, Paul's letters (which included Hebrews), 1 John, 1 Peter, and Revelation, although he makes further comments on Revelation, as we'll see.

The next category is those books that were widely accepted but disputed by some: James, Jude, 2 Peter, and 2 and 3 John. Eusebius

---

24. Philip Schaff and Henry Wace, eds., *Eusebius: Church History, Life of Constantine the Great, and Oration in Praise of Constantine*, vol. 1, A Select Library of the Nicene and Post-Nicene Fathers of the Christian Church, Second Series (New York: Christian Literature Company, 1890), 58.

himself doesn't seem to be among the disputers of these, although he had indicated he didn't trust 2 Peter in the past.

The third category is made of five "spurious" books: the Acts of Paul, the Shepherd of Hermas, the Apocalypse of Peter, the Letter of Barnabas, and the Didache. But oddly, he notes that some would disagree with him on Revelation, which he has already listed as accepted.

The volumes of Eusebius's history began to appear around the year 313, twelve years before the Council of Nicaea. When his first two categories are considered, attesting to a near-consensus among Christians, in his view, the conclusion must be that Christianity had a New Testament canon basically identical to the one used in the modern era. Up to this time, we find slight disagreements, particularly on the disputed books; *after* this time, we find almost no variance at all. It's not so much Eusebius's writing as it is the timing of it that's important here. At this juncture, for a number of reasons, the church was becoming of one mind, or very nearly so, in its evaluation of the Scriptures.

We can say that the great bulk of the canon was settled quite early, during the time of the Apostolic Fathers. The full canon, including Hebrews, Revelation, and the shorter letters, found acceptance by the beginning of the fourth century.

There's also the matter of Codex Sinaiticus and Codex Vaticanus, the two oldest of the four *great uncial codices*. These are early Greek collections of Scripture. The full, remarkable story of the Sinai version is told in Appendix B. The most complete ancient Bible in existence, it was created in the middle of the fourth century and demonstrates that the canon was all but complete. While it places Acts between Philemon and James, all of our current New Testament books are accounted for and in the right order. Two other books, Epistle of Barnabas and the Shepherd of Hermes, are placed at the end, where disputed or lesser writings were always included.

In 367, Athanasius of Alexandria released a "festal" letter setting forth all the dates for the popular Christian feasts of that year. This letter was an annual tradition in the Alexandrian church. But in this edition, he named the ultimately accepted twenty-seven books of the New Testament as exclusively canonical.

His purpose was to end the arguing once and for all about letters such the Shepherd of Hermas or the Epistle of Barnabas, which a few stubborn souls still advocated. At the same time, he wanted to affirm the authenticity of Peter's letters and Revelation, which a stubborn few still rejected. He wrote of the twenty-seven books, "In these alone the teaching of godliness is proclaimed. No one may add to them, and nothing may be taken away from them." This festal letter is thought to be the first formal and official statement of the final New Testament canon and the first to use that word in this context.

Augustine, bishop of Hippo in present-day Algeria, came along at about this time. A great many of the topics that he explored—free will, original sin, and the problem of evil, for example—are still approached in ways that Augustine first pioneered. In terms of the biblical canon, he was present in 393 when the twenty-seven books of the Christian New Testament were first officially stated. The records of that proceeding are lost, but a later council quoted the decision at Hippo that no other books were to be used in worship. Then, at the Sixth Council of Carthage in 419, the decision was reaffirmed and directed to the bishop of Rome and elsewhere in Christendom.[25]

At this point, especially with Jerome's translation of the Scriptures into Latin for what became the Latin Vulgate, nearly all churches began to follow this lead, accepting the twenty-seven books as inspired by God. Only in Syria was there widespread resistance against the disputed books for a longer period. This was also the beginning of the use of Latin in the church, gradually replacing the more informal and common language of Greek.

The New Testament was set and ready to be published together. Christianity had come into the world just as the Roman Empire was coming into its own. Now the latter declined as the former became

25. Howard Frederic Vos, *Exploring Church History* (Nashville, TN: Thomas Nelson Publishers, 1996), 198.

more powerful, more influential, and better defined through its Scriptures and church offices. Augustine, in *The City of God*, had the wisdom to separate the fate of a physical empire from that of a spiritual kingdom. The "City of God," he said, was supernatural and distinct from what was happening among princes and provinces.

That was certainly so, but it didn't mean that the church would be left unscathed by the massive transition the West was about to endure. A new age was beginning—what we refer to in common parlance as the Middle Ages. These centuries were arguably in the middle between the ancient and modern worlds, but were they "Dark Ages," as some attest?

Christianity kept the fire burning for reading, intellect, the arts, and spirituality. It would be called upon to provide light for those times, to be a "city of God" set upon a hill.

10

THE WORD SET FREE

Language is the ultimate barrier. The inability to speak to one another with understanding erects an immediate wall that is difficult to overcome.

In the fullness of time, to use the biblical phrase, the Mediterranean world was united by one common, smooth, and capable language, Koine Greek. Roman roads and common language created optimal conditions for spreading the Christian faith. People from three continents—Africa, Asia, and Europe—were able to converse. This ability to travel and speak a common tongue was quite helpful. Along with the later Christian canon, the Septuagint—the Bible in Greek—provided a common literature. Even with occasional persecution, doctrinal divisions, and other problems, the early years of the church were a time of rapid growth, the development of church structures, and a reasonable level of unity all across Christendom.

But after centuries of Roman rule, the fabric of Western civilization, the Roman Empire, was frayed and tearing apart. With a loss of central authority and the incursions of hostile tribes, the center did not hold, and Rome became politically weak. The East, home of Byzantine Christianity, was less affected and continued using the Greek language and some of the older traditions. Eastern Christians became less likely, however, to submit to church authorities in Rome, and Christendom gradually split into two geographical regions that evolved in different directions.

The Greek language became less common in Europe and Africa, and the years of Roman presence had made Latin more common as a shared language. The Western church, still based in Rome, used

Latin exclusively. This became another barrier with the Eastern church.

Jerome (347–420) was a theologian and writer who was born in what is now Slovenia in the mid-fourth century. He studied in Rome and wrote a great number of biblical commentaries. He had tried the monastic life, fascinated by the rigors of self-denial, but he was troubled by a dream in which he came before the throne of judgment and was accused of enjoying secular writings more than Christian ones. He redoubled his efforts to study the Hebrew language and Christian theology. He spent more time in the desert but found himself in too many arguments with various monks over the Trinity. Jerome hadn't found his destination.

Upon returning to Rome, he flourished. Jerome became an assistant to Pope Damasus I, bishop of Rome, and began a deeper study of the Scriptures and also wrote a great deal. In 382, the pope asked Jerome to revise the old Latin Bible. It had been around for a long time, and many faulty translated passages had been found; its Old Testament had been made from the Greek of the Septuagint, so it was a translation of a translation. Jerome's translation became known as the Latin Vulgate. *Vulgate* means common. In other words, this was a Bible for the common people, a forward-facing translation for a time when lay people could own and read Bibles.

The Vulgate has been called the most important of all the translations because the Roman church used it for so many centuries. Even today, there are ten thousand Vulgate translations in existence. Later, when the Bible was translated into other languages—German and French, for example—they were made from the Vulgate, then printed on Johannes Gutenberg's new printing press.[26] But that was centuries in the future. Jerome simply wanted an accurate Bible that everyone could read…provided that they read and spoke Latin. While he claimed his goal was to stick as closely to the older Latin text as possible, only changing what was clearly necessary, his final product

26. Bruce M. Metzger, *The Bible in Translation: Ancient and English Versions* (Grand Rapids, MI: Baker, 2001), 35.

was a superior translation, especially in the Gospels. Among other changes, he moved the order of the Gospels from Matthew, John, Luke, and Mark to the familiar order we use today. While Jerome's work was eventually used for nearly one thousand years, it only slowly gathered acceptance.

THE RISE OF THE PAPACY

What we think of as the Middle Ages covers a full millennium. It's generally considered to encompass the period from the late 400s to the late 1400s. No single chapter—no single book, for that matter—can begin to fully document the many activities of the church during what amounts to fifty percent of its history. Broad strokes will have to do.

As Europe in particular became less Roman, the church grew more Roman. The empire's fading power had left a vacuum, and the church was the only institution available to fill it. With Christianity blanketing a vast area similar to what the Roman Empire had encompassed, a more centralized and powerful church evolved to hold things together. It would seem that dominating Rome's world would be superior to being persecuted by it, but the church doesn't tend to flourish when it relies on political power. There was a great deal of corruption in the medieval church. In earlier days, all bishops and senior church leaders had the title of *pope*, but in time, this was reserved for the bishop of Rome. The idea of apostolic authority, beginning with Peter and handed down, now translated to the pope being Peter's heir and the ultimate authority.

The transitional figure was Gregory I, "Gregory the Great," in the late sixth century. He was a strong and strict administrator, as much like a Roman ruler as he was a bishop, and while he personally refused the title of pope, his writings show some of the first signs of many medieval Catholic developments, such as purgatory, the veneration of Mary, and praying to the saints. He also believed in full forgiveness of sins after repentance, confession, and penance, which helped lead to the Catholic confessional tradition.

His strong influence on the full network of churches helped to create a precedent that the bishop of Rome held the strongest authority. Yet Gregory also made important contributions to worship liturgy and music. The Gregorian Chant is named after him. He was a great believer in the verbal inspiration of Scripture, suggesting it really didn't matter who the authors of the books were because the true author was the Holy Spirit.

As a matter of fact, Gregory is often depicted in art accompanied by a dove. This comes from the legend that his assistant sat behind a screen writing as he dictated one of his scriptural commentaries. When there was a long pause, the assistant peeked through a hole in the screen and saw the Holy Spirit, in the form of a dove, placing the words into Gregory's mouth with his beak. Gregory was canonized as a saint and is one of the most celebrated of the popes.

As Muslims became aggressive in the Byzantine states beginning in the seventh century under Muhammad, Eastern Christianity was weakened as well. The medieval period continued, civilization became less urban and more rural, and the monarchs of each region began to have power over the local church, so that the lines between church and state blurred. This led to a great deal of corruption and compromise. In Rome, intrigue and bloodshed sometimes determined who became pope. Ecclesiastical posts were up for sale. In 1049, Leo IX made a tour of Europe to personally deal with immorality and corruption. He, too, is venerated as a saint and a consequential church leader, as is Thomas Aquinas.

Aquinas was a theologian the equal of Augustine. He hated the word *philosopher* because it signified a pagan who missed the truth revealed in Christ. Yet Aquinas was a philosopher of the first rank who studied the Greeks, particularly Aristotle, quite closely. Beyond deep study of Scripture and orderly thought on the nature of God, his wide-ranging beliefs included the concept of a just war, the place of politics, and capital punishment. His massive but incomplete *Summa Theologiae* presents five proofs for the existence of God.

Aquinas's most important work, however, was in his approach to the Bible. He rejected the idea that only the very educated or spiritually blessed could understand it. The Bible was for everyone, he maintained, and he made a strong case for reading it literally as opposed to allegorically, which was the favored way in the Middle Ages.

Allegorical interpretation may actually have begun with Origen, one of the early fathers. Origen read the thirty-third chapter of Numbers, which is a rather monotonous collection of sentences describing how the Israelites moved from one place to another. Forty-two different places are named. Origen couldn't understand why the Old Testament would give such prominence to a travel itinerary, so he decided the chapter was, in actuality, a description of forty-two stages of the Christian life. For him, this might also be symbolized by the forty-two generations connecting Abraham to Jesus, as detailed in the first chapter of Matthew.[27]

Medieval Christians adored Old Testament stories, in part because they were fascinated with the idea of puzzling out their *true meanings*. Difficult passages were explained as being mere symbols. If tribes were slaughtered, perhaps the true message was our personal war against sin. Beyond that, medieval people looked for allegories and symbols everywhere. The ark of the covenant was a symbol of the church, rescuing us from the flood of wickedness in the world. Jonah was in the great fish's belly for three days because he was a symbol of Christ, who was in the tomb for that long. Nearly every word or action of Joseph, the patriarch in Genesis, was interpreted symbolically.

Thomas Aquinas urged people to read the Bible in a more straightforward way. If God wanted to tell us something, He did so in plain language. He had nothing to hide. Aquinas's work had a wide-ranging influence in the Catholic church and, outside of that, upon philosophy in general.

---

27. Michal Hunt, "The Pentateuch Part IV: Numbers, Lesson 13: Chapters 33-36 The Summary of the stages of the Journey from Egypt to Israel's Last Encampment on the Banks of the Jordan River and The Conclusion of the Laws Prescribed on the Plains of Moab," Agape Bible Study, 2010, www.agapebiblestudy.com/Numbers/Numbers_Lesson_13.htm.

THE BIBLE BEYOND WORDS

It took centuries for Jerome's Latin Vulgate to become dominant, but Latin itself became the language of the church, even as local languages evolved and changed greatly during this period. English is a West Germanic language with Latin elements; Spanish and French evolved largely from Latin, with local influences. Languages, in general, moved on, but the written word doesn't change from what is written. As a result, the Latin Bible, whether Old Latin or Jerome's Vulgate, became less and less comprehensible to common people and was more the dialect of the church. In time, Latin was seen as a kind of *incantational* language that had something to do with prayers and invocations. The church viewed Latin as one of the three *sacred* languages, along with Hebrew and Greek.

The Bible wasn't necessarily inaccessible; wealthy families often owned them. However, by now, pages were made from vellum and animal skins, and the Bible required so many pages that the cost of possessing one was far too great for an ordinary family. On top of this, few could read or write, particularly in the Latin language of the Bible. On the other hand, the Bible was read quite often in church. The stories were told, but they were often told in Latin. Parts of the Bible were translated into Old English and Middle English.

The Bible was rarely taken as a whole. During the early portion of the Middle Ages, it existed primarily in two or three large folios. While thought leaders of the church had long since united the Scriptures by closing the canons, most people still thought of the Bible as a library of writings rather than a book.

As the calendar hit and passed the year 1000, Bibles became larger even as their exposure grew smaller. Monasteries used an Atlantic Bible, which consisted of massive volumes set on lecterns. Yet because of the size, certain sections—even the Psalms and the Gospels—might be left out. These Bibles were created for the sake of appearance: they made a statement. But the idea of the Bible as an object of art was in keeping with the birth of the illuminated manuscript, which featured Bible pages with much more than words.

Illustrations were hand-created and painted. Inks of different colors were used for chapters or headings. Beautiful fonts were used. To be *illuminated*, a manuscript had to contain some kind of metal, such as gold or silver leaf. These started out as the product of monasteries, but became popular among wealthy patrons, who often had the Bibles personalized. Christian devotional books known as "books of hours" inspired the reader with psalms, prayers, and stories throughout the hours of the day.

Even as the words of the Bible became inaccessible to many common people, something remarkable—and perhaps instructive—happened. The Word broke through without using words. The Middle Ages began a period of remarkable religious arts. If people couldn't read, they could gaze upon windows that depicted Bible stories in breathtaking color.

For example, there are 176 windows in Chartres Cathedral in France, which was completed in 1252. They begin with the story of Adam and Eve, proceed through highlights of the Old Testament, and then fully illustrate the story of Jesus. (They also show the occupations of local patrons who helped to pay for the windows.)

Liturgical feasts at Christmas, Easter, and Epiphany used music, drama, and poetry to tell the stories of sin and redemption. Easter plays showed the story of the crucifixion and resurrection dramatically, but these grew into passion plays that often showed highlights of the life of Jesus. And beyond these works, a surprising amount of theatrical art was used in the service of Christianity. Morality plays, mystery plays, and miracle plays were all popular productions that showed aspects of Christian life or Bible stories. Mystery plays depicted stories from the Bible with simple vocal musical accompaniment. Miracle plays depicted the lives of the saints, while morality plays showed symbolic stories about life, temptation, and redemption.

Meanwhile, monks in the monasteries began to develop new forms of vocal music for use in worship, from monophonic chants to heterophonic and polyphonic developments that experimented with melody to express worship of God. Much of the Western music tradition grew out of what began in medieval worship.

It's interesting to note that we have the names of only a few of the artists, musicians, or playwrights behind these works. During the Renaissance era that followed the Middle Ages, the artists' names took on importance and pride, though their works were devoted to sacred subjects. Michelangelo, for instance, carved the lovely *Pietà*, showing Mary holding the body of her crucified Son. But when the sculptor heard that his work had been credited to another artist, he grew angry and added boastful words across Mary's sash reading, "Michelangelo Buonarroti, the Florentine, made this."

In medieval times, such a thing was impossible; the spiritual lesson was all that mattered. The artists, great as their craft may be, didn't sign their work at all. Even today, those who enter the massive medieval cathedrals suddenly feel tiny. Inside or outside, the lines of the cathedral move upward and direct the eyes toward heaven. This was the view of humanity during the trials of the Middle Ages. People were small and temporary. Life was difficult, and a peasant would never be more than a peasant. But the church directed people's spirits toward heaven, toward hope. And if the Bible could not be read, God, through inspired artists, delivered His message in new ways—through visible art, music, storytelling, and theater.

God's message can be stifled at times. It can be suppressed in places. It can be distorted. It can be ignored. It can be banned or burned. But it can't be permanently destroyed or detoured from its journey through time as humanity's lifeline. As the prophet Isaiah notes, "*The word of our God stands forever*" (Isaiah 40:8).

THE LIGHT OF DAWN

It was inevitable that a massive culture shift would begin at some point after centuries of the various regressions of the Middle Ages. One way of looking at it—an admittedly simplistic one—would be that the medieval arts encouraged by the church led to the phenomenal growth of artistic expression of the Renaissance, and the sophisticated explorations of men such as Thomas Aquinas pointed toward the revival of classicism and learning that broke out in the fifteenth century. It's not simplistic at all to suggest that the overreach and arrogance of the Catholic Church in the late Middle Ages, when it became quite corrupt, led to the Protestant Reformation.

While the transition was more gradual than it's often depicted, it did seem as if the Western world awoke from a long slumber and was suddenly full of energy. And that energy extended to a demand for the Bible.

John Wycliffe (1330–1384) has been called "the morning star of the Reformation." The Englishman had a deep resentment toward what he thought was a church that overstepped its bounds. He had a number of doctrinal disagreements with Rome, and one of them was that people were deprived of reading the Bible in their own language rather than one that was either dead or dying. In particular, he felt he'd have more people on his side if they could read how the Scriptures supported his argument. There was nothing in the Bible about needing the mediation of bishops or cardinals to enter the gates of heaven. These views had crept into the faith over time. As a matter of fact, he believed that the truth of the Scriptures was in itself enough for salvation, without any blessing of the church.

Wycliffe took it upon himself to translate the Bible into English for the first time, though he focused mainly on the New Testament. He wasn't fluent in Greek or Hebrew, so he and his assistant, John Purvey, worked from the Latin and completed the New Testament in 1380, with Purvey taking the lead on the Old Testament and completing that two years later. Then gathering some of his "Lollard" followers, as they were dubbed in derision (the word meant "babblers"), the group was dispatched throughout England to preach a biblical gospel. The effect was strong, but much more powerful was Wycliffe's future influence. Years after his death, his enemies dug up his body, held a "trial" condemning him for heresy, and then burned the remains.

Meanwhile, a studious follower of Wycliffe created an improved version of the English translation that was soon in circulation.

Over in Bohemia, the western region of current Czech Republic, Wycliffe's beliefs and writings were known and admired a generation later. A priest and professor, Jan Huss, studied Wycliffe and Scripture and found himself in agreement. After he traveled to study claims of miracles in various churches, he wrote a work criticizing the *miracle industry* and urging Christians to live by the revealed truth of the Bible rather than depending upon the sensational.

It was politics, of a sort, that got Huss in trouble. During this period, there were two claimants to the office of pope. The position Huss took pleased the local government but made enemies in the church. He was more frequently criticized for being a follower of Wycliffe and attacking the selling of indulgences. Eventually, Huss was imprisoned, tried for heresy, and burned as a heretic in 1415. But again, martyrdom energized ordinary Christians who admired Jan Huss, and throughout Europe, conditions were present for the massive ecclesiastical eruptions that followed almost a century later.

LUTHER IGNITES A REVOLUTION

The story has been told countless times, but it never loses its powerful drama. What could have been dry ecclesiastical history became a worldwide spectacle.

The year was 1516. St. Peter's Basilica, the traditional burial site of Peter, was being rebuilt in Rome. The Italian Renaissance was in full flower, and architecture of this type was expected to be sensational and expensive. Pope Leo X sent a friar named Johann Tetzel to Germany to sell indulgences to raise funds. Indulgences amounted to remission from punishment in the afterlife for oneself or one's loved ones, sold for a price. This had become a common strategy that transformed people's fears of eternal punishment into financial gain for the church. Tetzel even had a jingle of sorts: "A coin into the coffer rings, a soul from purgatory springs!"

On October 31, 1517, a young German priest and professor, Martin Luther, sent a document containing ninety-five theses, or theological assertions, to his bishop. The gist of the presentation was that indulgences were found nowhere in Scripture, and the church had no say-so in matters of eternal punishment. The famous story is that Luther nailed these theses to the door of his church at Wittenberg, but some scholars take this to be mere legend. From that small beginning, a massive movement unfurled.

If not for a recent invention, also in Germany, Martin Luther's name might be long since forgotten. But Johannes Gutenberg, in Mainz, had introduced an ingenious mechanism known as the movable metal type printing press. This meant hand-copying manuscripts—especially lengthy ones such as the Bible—was a thing of the past. In 1455, Gutenberg printed forty-two copies of the Bible, based on the Latin Vulgate. Ironically, he also printed thousands of indulgences for the church.

By 1517, printing presses were cranking out books and papers of all kinds. Luther's ninety-five theses quickly gained wide distribution and created an outcry. Soon, Luther's name came before the most powerful church authorities in Rome.

Luther happened to be a very serious-minded Christian—some would say a tormented one. He worried constantly about his own salvation. He prayed, he read, he questioned everything. At some point, he found the works of John Wycliffe in a library and puzzled over why such a good and virtuous man should have been condemned by so many. Later, while studying Romans, he had a moment of epiphany. He understood that salvation came fully through the grace of God, a gift, and that the works-based traditions he had learned were irrelevant and false. Luther later wrote, "I felt as if I were entirely born again, and had entered paradise itself through the gates that had been flung open."[28]

---

28. Mark Galli and Ted Olsen, eds., "Martin Luther," in *131 Christians Everyone Should Know* (Nashville, TN: Broadman & Holman Publishers, 2000), 34–35.

Even so, soul-searching introversion continued to be his nature. So did stubbornness. And when he was called upon to recant, he wouldn't budge. In public debate, Luther declared that a layman with a Bible was the equal of pope and councils without one. He was told he was facing excommunication from the church, which in the church's estimation amounted to being condemned to hell.

Luther again benefited from the printing press when he released several more tracts. His greatest theme was salvation by grace alone, but he also said that every Christian was a priest, and just as shockingly, he reduced the sacraments from seven to two: baptism and communion. These are all claims that became popular during the Reformation.

He appeared before the Holy Roman emperor, Charles V, and refused to recant. Unless someone could show him good reasons, he said, "Here I stand—God help me."

Before he could be arrested and tried, he was whisked to Wartburg Castle, where he hid for almost a year, translating the New Testament into German in only eleven weeks, and also writing hymns for German commoners in their own language. Two prominent Wittenberg merchants hired a printer to run as many copies of the German New Testament through the printer as possible. A popular book fair was coming in Leipzig. Extra presses were brought in. As many as five thousand copies were completed and packaged for sale, and the edition was a huge hit. Every single copy was sold.[29]

This was the moment the Bible—at least in New Testament form—became the bestselling book in existence. As a matter of fact, even the unscrupulous took notice, printing and selling pirated copies. Over a year's time, there were twelve authorized and sixty-six unauthorized reprints of the German New Testament. Germans, with their love of lengthy compound words, know this as the *Septembertestament*, referring to the date of the book fair.

---

29. Erik Herrmann, "'And they will all be taught of God': Martin Luther's Biblical Translation at 500," ConcordiaTheology, September 30, 2022, concordiatheology. org/2022/09/and-they-will-all-be-taught-of-god-martin-luthers-biblical-translation-at-500.

Luther's Bible translation had the same effect as the King James Version in English—it became so familiar in its language that many of his chosen phrases became common phrases in German. Luther's controversial reputation didn't hurt sales. Neither did the fact that his edition cost the buyer a small fraction of what Gutenberg's Latin Bible had cost.

After he left the castle, Luther's populist movement had become so popular that he couldn't be touched. Not only that, but it had spread into other countries. John Calvin became a powerful leader in Geneva. Reformation ideas caught fire in England during the time of King Henry VIII. And the Bible began to be translated into all the main languages, as people everywhere demanded a Bible to read for themselves.

Luther never intended to start a denomination and certainly not a competing branch of Christianity. His personal religion remained quite Catholic, with the exception of the scriptural doctrines about which he was passionate. As he studied the Bible, he came to the conclusion that nothing in it forbade him from marrying, and he took a wife.

Regardless of his intentions, a denomination—Lutheranism— did form around him, and Presbyterianism formed around John Calvin. The Church of England became separate from the Roman Catholic Church. And all this was just the beginning. The Protestant movement stressed the priesthood of every believer, Scripture as the prime authority (*Sola scriptura*), and salvation by grace.

A few years later, Rome responded through the Council of Trent, which convened over a number of years and responded to what was known as the Protestant Reformation. It did condemn some of the abuses that had occurred, but it also affirmed the authority of the church and the Latin Vulgate as the preferred translation, as opposed to the languages people spoke. It condemned what it saw as heresies by the Protestants.

This was a time when explorers such as Ferdinand Magellan, Christopher Columbus, and Vasco da Gama were setting out by sea to explore the world; when science was making important breakthroughs through men like Sir Isaac Newton, Nicolaus Copernicus, and Galileo Galilei; when Leonardo Da Vinci and Michelangelo were creating art; and when the Gregorian calendar was introduced. In short, the dawn was breaking out after a long, dark night of Western humanity. The arts of printing, binding, and distribution were improving every day, and the book people wanted the most was the Bible. The great age of Bible translation began—an age that has yet to end.

11

IN PLAIN ENGLISH

It's natural to assume the Protestant Reformation brought forth a flood of Bible translations, and this is at least partly true. The entire Bible was printed in fifteen European languages by 1600.[30]

But several of those were already in distribution before the Reformation was in full bloom. According to some scholars, it's more accurate to reverse the equation: letting people understand the Bible was the single spark for the Reformation. However, the translation trend didn't fade out once these nationalities had their Bible. It only began a process that has continued to this day.

Language is ephemeral. In the great scheme of things, it lives for a season, like the butterfly. The message of God, on the other hand, is eternal and changeless; it never ages or withers.

So as languages transform, taking on new words and styles while shedding others like cocoons, the Word must find new homes. Each generation deserves a Bible that speaks its language with perfect fluency. As a result, there are always scholars and linguists working together, mastering the original languages, and finding the best contemporary words to carry that age-old message forward into this new dawn.

William Tyndale (1495–1536), who lived in England during the Reformation, was one of those scholars. He knew from an early age that his life's work was to create a better translation of the Bible in the English language. He once spoke with a church official who told him that laypeople had no need to read the Bible, that the clergy could

---

30. "A brief history of Bible translation," Wycliffe Bible Translators, wycliffe.org.uk/story/a-brief-history-of-bible-translation.

interpret it for them. Tyndale replied, "If God should spare my life, before many years, I will cause the boy that drives the plow to know more of the Scripture than you do."[31] His words encompassed the spirit of the Protestant Reformation. People were learning to read; they were eager to think, ask questions, and explore God's Word for themselves.

Tyndale avoided the earlier work by Wycliffe because he wanted the language to be new and contemporary. Wycliffe's translation is now considered Middle English, while Tyndale's is classified as Early Modern English. This was one of those periods in which language transformed rapidly, and Tyndale understood that.

Erasmus, the Dutch theologian, had created a new, more accurate Greek New Testament, known as the *Textus Receptus* ("received text"). Tyndale and Martin Luther both made use of it in their work. Wycliffe had worked secondhand, from the Latin Vulgate. For centuries, the Erasmus text was viewed as the most accurate and reliable work.

England had not yet made its break with Rome, so Tyndale's work was not welcomed by the local church. He had to lay low in Germany for years as he worked on his New Testament and some of the Old. Fifteen thousand Tyndale New Testaments had been smuggled into England, regardless of the government's attempts to stop it. An awaiting audience was overjoyed.

Tyndale never completed his Old Testament, although his assistant Miles Coverdale did and went on to release a full Bible. By this time, Tyndale had been tracked down, imprisoned in a castle in Brussels, Belgium, and tried for heresy. It wasn't always the act of Bible translation that infuriated the church; it was more about the pesky notes in the margin. Tyndale included annotations to the text that took strong theological positions and missed no opportunity to hurl accusations at the Roman Catholic Church. In 1536, Tyndale

---

31. P. M. Bechtel and P. W. Comfort, "Tyndale, William," in *Who's Who in Christian History*, eds. J. D. Douglas and Philip W. Comfort (Wheaton, IL: Tyndale House, 1992), 684.

was strangled and burned at the stake, with his last words being, "Lord, open the King of England's eyes."[32]

The king, it so happened, was Henry VIII. The extent to which his eyes were opened (in Tyndale's sense) is questionable, but the time arrived when he was sponsoring Bible translations of his own—translations that made use of Tyndale's excellent work. As is well-known, Henry's break with the church was less a matter of theology than his eagerness for a divorce that the pope would not grant. Yet as things played out, Tyndale's prayer may have been answered. Only three years after his martyrdom, a Bible appeared with a large illustration of King Henry on its cover, though Oliver Cromwell deserved most of the credit.

DUELING BIBLES

Henry VIII commissioned an English Bible to be read in church, and he appointed none other than Miles Coverdale, the protégé of Tyndale, for the work.

Coverdale had spent a great deal of time in exile in Germany, and his mentor had been executed. Now Coverdale was completing his work for the executioners. However, the Church of England's primary concern was not getting the Word of God to the people but—if they *must* have a Bible—giving them one free of the offensive annotations Tyndale had added. However, Coverdale didn't work from the original languages. He wasn't the scholar Tyndale had been. He translated from the Latin Vulgate and German. When this flaw became obvious, it helped to spur the later Bishops' Bible into production.

All churches in England were required to own one of these Bibles and read from it. The copy was kept chained to the lectern to prevent it from being stolen. Some people later referred to it as "the chained Bible" for that reason, though it had other names. The one that stuck was the Great Bible, due to its hefty size. While this Bible was favored

---

32. Steven Lawson, "William Tyndale's Final Words," Ligonier Ministries, February 18, 2015, www.ligonier.org/learn/articles/william-tyndales-final-words.

for only a brief period, high quality editions were printed, with hand-colored woodcut illustrations. Much of the English prayerbook is inspired by this translation. Henry VIII's personal copy is on display at the British Library in London. These special editions were used to make the Bible more attractive than its competing versions, and no doubt helped to fan interest in the Scriptures.

During its brief period of popularity, more people began reading the Bible and repeating its language, which seemed to offend the king. Henry VIII believed that the church was the place for Bible verses and the sacred words of Scripture shouldn't be "disputed, rimed, sung, and jangled in every alehouse."[33] After a time, the king restricted usage of the Bible to the wealthy class. Then, when he prohibited all other versions, the size of the Great Bible made it impractical for common people. If the Great Bible failed, the biggest reason was the fickleness of the king himself.

Next came the Geneva Bible, a far more memorable production. Queen Mary, the daughter of Catherine of Aragon, was now on the throne. She was a Catholic who restored England to its former allegiance to Rome during her short reign. Predictably, this abrupt change of a nation's religion created chaos and bloodshed, thus earning the queen the moniker "Bloody Mary." The dangers of the period drove translators and serious students into exile, and in Geneva, they fell under the spell of John Calvin and his majestic vision of the omnipotent God. The resulting Bible made a massive impact. Shakespeare used this Bible. The Mayflower settlers had several copies aboard, some of which have survived. The Geneva Bible was the Bible of Oliver Cromwell and his Separatist followers during the English Civil War.

One of the significant factors of the Geneva Bible was that it was offered straight from the printing press to anyone who wanted to buy it—and at an affordable price. Up until then, Bibles had been offered to churches, though at times common people owned copies. The Geneva Bible became the firm favorite of private book-buyers.

---

33. "History of the Bible," Historical Bible Society, accessed May 19, 2023, www.historicalbiblesociety.org/history-of-the-bible.

As if mere availability weren't enough, this Bible was loaded with the same kinds of features that fine study Bibles contain in the twenty-first century. Each Bible book offered an introduction. There were maps, tables, annotations, and plenty of cross-references, so that an important verse might offer the reference to a related verse—and this was only possible because the Geneva Bible was the first edition to divide the text into both chapters and verses.

The versification of Scripture was a crucial moment in Bible history. At first glance, the miniscule numbers appearing amid the words of the Bible must have seemed odd, even ungainly. But they revolutionized Bible studies; one could cite the specific location of a verse, and the chapter numbers provided helpful milestones for quickly navigating to a passage. These had been added in the early 1200s at the University of Paris. The new system of chapter-and-verse took hold quickly, so that new versions of the Bible nearly always used it.

These features encouraged a deeper level of study and devotion. Again, there were woodcut illustrations, very often graphic and eye-opening. The Great Bible didn't seem particularly great anymore, and it didn't go unnoticed when English people were seen with copies of this Swiss import rather than their own, royally approved Bible— which, by the way, was published in smaller, more convenient editions and cost less than a week's pay for the working class.

Most worrisome of all, from the point of view of English royalty, was that the Great Bible again offered annotations that went far beyond stated biblical truth. The notes took Puritan positions derived from Calvinism and sometimes challenged the authority of kings and princes, though never with as much impudence as Tyndale had shown.

BISHOP TO KING

The Bishops' Bible is seldom remembered today. Its appearance was brief, and it was overshadowed by the massively successful translation that followed it. It was also quite a bland production.

The Bishops' Bible followed the Great Bible by less than thirty years. More relevantly, it followed the Geneva Bible, which was unauthorized but quite popular. It had appeared only eight years prior, and it worried the powers that be. This Geneva Bible had been produced by a new form of Christianity, the Presbyterians, who actually suggested that ordinary laypeople should govern the church, instead of a hierarchy of bishops. That was more Reformation than the Church of England wanted, to say the least. Elizabeth, the daughter of Henry VIII and Anne Boleyn, was on the throne by now, replacing her half-sister, and she had just as abruptly restored the Church of England as the state religion. It was time for a fresh start and a new Bible.

The Archbishop of Canterbury proposed one. Perhaps the reason for the poor product produced was the lack of vision. Rather than being driven by a passion for an effective and inspiring reflection of God's Word, the purpose of this Bible production was reactive, an effort to replace something uncomfortable. Neither was the Bishops' Bible well organized. The duties of translation were divided, and the bishops who did the translating worked separately rather than together. The styles of individual books clashed. The two primary Hebrew references to God, YHWH and Elohim, were translated as "God" and "the Lord," respectively, in some books, and the opposite way in others.

In some places, the Geneva Bible phrasings were copied very closely; in others, the translation was a great departure. The Psalms had little sense of rhythm and music, so that the individual psalms were extremely difficult to set to melody for worship. This was a significant problem because the intent of the Bishops' Bible was church use. It couldn't compete with the Geneva Bible for the customers who wanted a Bible for their homes, but this Bible was the one approved for worship. It was called the Bishops' Bible for that reason—it was the one the bishops created and then insisted upon in church.

This version simply lacked the poetic beauty of other translations, especially the King James Version that followed it very quickly.

In modernized English, here is how the Bishops' Bible began Psalm 23:

> God is my shepherd, therefore I can lack nothing:
>
> He will cause me to repose myself in pasture full of grass, and he will lead me unto calm waters.

Technically, this is a perfectly acceptable translation of the Hebrew. But compare the same verses in the King James Version:

> *The LORD is my shepherd; I shall not want. He maketh me to lie down in green pastures: he leadeth me beside the still waters.*
>
> (Psalm 23:1–2 KJV)

We take for granted the familiar old style of the King James, accepting it as "the way they talked in those days." But it's something closer to "the way they wrote poetry." Notice the use of *maketh* and *leadeth* to create rhythm. The Bishops' Bible doesn't use "eth" forms in its translation of these verses. Perhaps after a few years of hearing bishops drone through psalms with flat diction, the translators who succeeded them envisioned a Bible that would read well, recite well, and sing well on Sunday morning. Anyone who has ever recited the Lord's Prayer from Matthew 6 or Psalm 23 in church recognizes the easy rhythm found by a congregation, speaking the words together quietly:

> *Our Father which art in heaven,*
>
> *Hallowed be thy name.*
>
> *Thy kingdom come,*
>
> *Thy will be done*
>
> *in earth, as it is in heaven.*   (Matthew 6:9–10)

The "long" syllables are underlined. Poets recognize this short-long, short-long style as *iambic* meter. Wherever possible, the translators of the King James Version created these rhythms, providing musicality to the material, particularly in the Psalms or other passages meant to be spoken or sung. It lodges easily in the memory in ways newer translations do not, so that we find Scripture is more difficult to memorize than in days when most people used the King James.

One of the more famous translations of the Bishops' Bible is Ecclesiastes 11:1. It rendered the first part of the verse as, "Lay thy bread upon wette faces." The King James, only a few short years later, gave us, "*Cast thy bread upon the waters.*" Even prior to our understanding of that verse's meaning, we're attracted to the music of the words.

The translators of the Bishops' Bible missed these nuances; the next group of translators didn't.

Meanwhile, the Roman Catholic scholars released an English Bible of their own in their desire to counter what they charged as heresy in the new Protestant Bibles. This whole business of translating the Scriptures could be very controversial. For example, the word *bishop* occurs in the New Testament. The Greek word is *episkopos*, and Protestant translations would often use the generic word *overseer*.

Catholics insisted that this word was to be translated as *bishop*—an assertion suggesting that the Catholic offices and hierarchy were right there in the Bible. They were infuriated to see these words reinterpreted in ways that seemed to challenge Catholic authority. But now Protestants could bring out their English-language Bibles, point to a verse, and say, "Here's what the Bible says." Catholics needed something to fight back with.

The Douay-Rheims Bible, produced by Catholic scholars and named for the two French universities where it was created, used the Latin Vulgate as its source and remained as close to it as possible. Given the fears of rampant Protestant beliefs, a great many of the verse translations were given theological coloring, so that, for instance, John the Baptist came preaching "the baptism of penance" rather than repentance. A great many textual notes sought to ensure a Catholic understanding of the passages. The New Testament was released in 1582, with the full Bible appearing a few years later. With Queen Elizabeth, a Protestant, on the throne, the Douay-Rheims Bible was severely limited in its market, but it did give Catholic loyalists a Bible they could read in English.

All of these Bibles were something new and wonderous to ordinary churchgoers. The Bible had been something they'd been around, heard about, and knew to some extent. They saw it as the authority for life, truth, and morals. Yet now they could see the words and, if they were literate, read them for themselves. In Essex, an anonymous writer recorded that "poor men bought the New Testament of Jesus Christ and on Sundays did sit reading in the lower end of the church, and many would flock about them to hear their reading."[34]

A BIBLE FOR THE AGES

The King James who took the throne of England in 1603 is formally referred to as King James VI and I, because he had first been the Scottish king and now united the countries under one monarch. England and Scotland did retain their own parliaments, but having a single monarch was significant.

James was a careful ruler. He seemingly had no powerful doctrinal feelings apart from the idea that all rulers were appointed by God and held divine rights; they were accountable only to heaven. But James did care deeply about avoiding explosive conflict. So he listened to both Puritans and Catholics, tolerating both as much as possible. If he could just keep peace between various factions, he could avoid conspiracies and assassination plots—of which there were several from the beginning.

It was John Reynolds, a Puritan from Oxford, who brought forward the idea of a Bible translation that all parties could use. This would seem to be a high goal, but it was true that the Bishops' Bible held sway over the churches and clergy, while the Geneva Bible was by

34. David M. Scholer, "How We Got Our Bible: Did You Know?", Christian History Institute, accessed May 19, 2023, christianhistoryinstitute.org/magazine/article/how-we-got-our-bible-did-you-know.

far the favorite of laypeople. King James was keen on the idea of being a force for unity, and he was attracted to the possibility of replacing the church's Bible *and* the family's Bible with one new work. So he sponsored what was called the Authorized Version but has always been better known as the King James Bible.

The king called for a version that represented the best of the previous Bibles and could be read in any environment. He had one strong stipulation: *stick to the text.* He disliked the intrusive annotations and notes that brought biases and political matters into church. Tyndale's Bible had been quite vocal about the place of kings and princes, and James insisted on curtailing the textual notes.

James followed the sensible pattern of the Geneva Bible, as much as he disliked it, and chose a revision committee. Fifty-four men were selected in the beginning, forty-seven of whom actually worked on the Bible. They were divided into groups: one working on Chronicles through Ecclesiastes plus the Apocrypha; two groups taking on Isaiah through Malachi, the four gospels, Acts, and Revelation; and two translating Genesis through 2 Kings and Romans through Jude. These groups were divided between Cambridge, Oxford, and Westminster.

The improved organization corrected some of the problems with the Bishops' Bible, which had suffered from poor coordination and communication. There was agreement on which previous translations to favor for various textual issues. The Bishops' Bible was used as the preliminary source, but the translators strove for the kind of precise wording they saw in the Geneva Bible.

As has been noted, a world of familiar modern expressions are associated with this Bible, even four hundred years later. However, it's easy to forget that the King James translators didn't devise all these terms. Many actually came from Tyndale and other sources. Even Wycliffe before him coined a number of words and phrases, and the King James Version merely picked them up. The version of YHWH that is spelled *Jehovah* comes from Tyndale. So do "cast the first stone" and "eat, drink, and be merry." "My cup runneth over" and "get thee behind me, Satan" are products of the Geneva Bible. So all of these translations made contributions to the direction of the English language. It's the Bible itself, rather than any particular version, that has had such a powerful impact on the way we think and speak.

But there's no question that the King James Bible towers above the other efforts of the time. Most scholars of the 1611 Bible note several reasons this Bible has showed such staying power:

+ **The committee was well-chosen.** These were the best biblical scholars of the age. During a time when there was a great passion for learning, they took their work seriously, cooperated well, and produced an excellent work.

+ **Cooperation between king, state, and church**—and the desire to create one non-divisive Bible—kept the translators from scholarly abuses. Throughout the Bible, the translators put objective scholarship first. If the king wanted to place a certain slant on words having to do with government and authority, the scholars refused. Bias may have crept in here or there, but not nearly as much as in past translations.

+ **The work of all previous translators** was now available for this work. The Bishops' Bible was the foundation, but the Geneva Bible, the Great Bible, and the Tyndale Bible could all be mined for contribution. There was a great desire to surpass all of those prior works.

+ **Lessons of organization learned from the Geneva Bible** had a great impact. In the days of Wycliffe and even Tyndale, a small group of men (at most) had set out to translate the entire Bible. "Dividing and conquering" was a better approach, both for efficiency and for mutual checks and balances.

+ **The Age of Shakespeare** certainly created a love for poetry and the music of language that affected how words were assembled to create verses and passages. Not only was William Shakespeare still alive in 1611, but Christopher Marlowe, Edmund Spenser, and John Donne were among those who penned plays and poems during this time. Was Shakespeare somehow involved in the translation of the King James Bible? That's the rumor, and it's tempting, if utterly unsupported by evidence. In any case, the reasoning is that Shakespeare was forty-six years old in 1611. Check the nearest King James Version or *New King James* edition, and you'll find that the forty-sixth word of Psalm 46 is "shake" (in verse 3) and the forty-sixth word from the end (in verse 9) is "spear." Was it a coincidence, or a King James "Easter egg" to thank the bard for his help on the Psalms?[35]

A unique, common language (Greek) had been used to spread the gospel. Now, with equally perfect timing, the English language, at its peak of beauty and expression, was employed to create a powerful and enduring Bible.

It's not that the translators were necessarily attempting to write poetically. If they had, their efforts would no doubt have been labored and false. The king never delivered any mandate for a Bible that was beautiful to read; he wanted clarity without controversy. He wanted his country to settle on one Bible, once and for all.

But he got a great deal more. Listen to the opening words of the King James Bible with fresh ears:

> *In the beginning God created the heaven and the earth. And the earth was without form, and void; and darkness was upon the face of the deep. And the Spirit of God moved upon the face of the waters. And God said, Let there be light: and there was light.*   (Genesis 1:1–3 KJV)

There's nothing pretentious about these lines; they're straightforward and tell the story. But the difference between this and past Bibles is the difference between "cast thy bread upon wet faces" and the magnificent line, *"Darkness was upon the face of the deep."* This is followed by the equally transcendent, *"And the Spirit of God moved*

---

35. Kyle Butt, "Did Shakespeare Slip His Name in Psalm 46?", Apologetics Press, accessed May 19, 2023, apologeticspress.org/did-shakespeare-slip-his-name-in-psalm-46-925.

upon the face of the waters." There is alliteration at the perfect moment: *"Let there be light."* And we find internal rhyme in *"without form and void."*

Recent translations read fairly similarly, but the King James Version perfected the rhythm and music of the verses.

FINE-TUNING THE LANGUAGE

Bibles are almost never one-and-done printings. They go through several revisions over time. Just during its first year, the King James Version had three editions. It was available in various sizes. But printing presses aren't as perfect as they may seem. In arranging and rearranging the type, just as much error was invited as if scribes had been hand-copying the words.

The most famous printing error occurred in a 1631 edition, when the Tenth Commandment was printed without that meaningful little word, "not." Thus, "Thou shalt commit adultery" was right there on the page as a commandment from Mt. Sinai. This gaffe gained that edition infamy (and a bit of snickering) as the "Wicked Bible." Another Bible substituted the word *vinegar* for *vineyard.* In what quickly became known as the "Murderer's Bible," Jesus said, "Let the children first be killed" instead of "filled" in Mark 7:27.

While the King James Version has retained its popularity, it has done so with the help of updated spelling on many occasions over the years. Benjamin Blayney's name is far more important than most students of the Bible realize. He made tens of thousands of small changes, according to some scholars. Then, in 1870, the Church of England commissioned another large-scale revision of the aging Bible, now going on 260 years old. This revision was done by more than fifty scholars ranging across many denominations, though anchored by Anglicans, and the result was highly successful. It was known as the *Revised Version* in England. Americans had some input and were able to release the *American Standard Edition,* as they called it, in 1901.

Most Bible owners were unaware of all these revisions and language tweaks. They happily read their King James Bibles, and their children did the same, and so did their grandchildren. The purpose of King James for his commissioned Bible was to unite English-speaking Christendom with one Bible. He couldn't have imagined the remarkable extent to which this book would do just that for centuries, so that most people quoted and memorized verses in perfect synchronization.

The growth of the United States increased the market for the King James Bible, but for a while, it was hard to come by. After the Revolutionary War, American relations with England weren't positive, and shipments of the Bible were cut off. Isaac Collins, a print shop owner in Trenton, New Jersey, wanted to know why the new nation should depend upon Bible imports in the first place. The great Book could be printed on these shores. His proposal: if he could be guaranteed a 25 percent deposit from no fewer than three thousand subscribers, he could finance a printing of the Bible.

That goal was easily surpassed. Collins began organizing the mammoth undertaking—all of the text had to be freshly set—and hired as many proofreaders as he could find, including his own children. He said they read the Bible eleven times looking for typos. After two years of work, he managed full plates for a Bible press run that contained exactly two errors: a misplaced punctuation mark and a broken letter. For many years, the Collins Bible was considered the most typographically accurate Bible yet published. Collins initiated one variance from British editions: he left out the dedication to King James, which he felt added nothing in terms of edification and was possibly even improper.

Just as important, it pioneered a new phenomenon: the "family Bible," which was soon found on the shelves of nearly every proud family. These editions were usually oversized, well-illustrated, handsome, and always in the King James Version. The original Collins Bibles have become something of a collector's item, with fewer than one hundred copies surviving. Family Bibles are valuable for genealogists, who consult the family trees often inscribed in the fly-leaf. Family notes, photographs, and recipes can also be found tucked into the hefty pages.

Family Bibles carried great symbolism. To place one prominently in a household made a statement about values, and to list the family tree inside tied father, mother, children, and others ever tightly to the Scriptures. Many generations of children came of age studying the vivid illustrations with rapt interest.

As the English language changed, as it was always bound to do, this translation only took on more dignity. As an aging but beloved text, it had a classic sound to it—not surprisingly, like Shakespeare. Younger students, upon encountering a more modern Bible for the first time, were often incredulous: didn't Jesus Himself speak in thees and thous?

Presidents and other politicians used the King James as their model, not simply quoting it but attempting to co-opt its high style. Abraham Lincoln could simply have said the number eighty-seven in his Gettysburg Address and saved everyone a little mental mathematics; instead, he said, "Four score and seven years ago," giving biblical heft to his words. Martin Luther King Jr.'s famous "I have a dream" speech is loaded with allusions to the Psalms and the Prophets.

In the middle of the twentieth century, however, there developed an appetite for less gravitas and more informality in Bible reading. In 1937, the International Council of Religious Education made the point that biblical scholarship had made significant strides since the seventeenth century. There was a better understanding of the ancient languages. There had been archaeological breakthroughs. People wanted a new Bible that would reflect all that we'd come to understand, while still honoring the high literary standards of the King James Version. This was the beginning of what became the *Revised Standard Version*.

The twenty-two elite scholars worked from the *American Standard Version*, still relatively new at the time, and established rules. *Thee* and *thy* disappeared unless they were in reference to God. Sentences were rearranged more clearly.

World War II delayed the full Bible until 1952, being the first Bible translation to make use of the Dead Sea Scrolls. It was released to mixed reactions. Many were delighted; others felt that attempting to replace the King James Version was like daring to replace the Bible itself; the two had become synonymous. There were arguments over prophetic language in the Old Testament. But a great many churches began using this version.

A brand-new version, the *New Revised Standard Version,* was released in 1989. But by this time, a new Bible was hardly front-page news. A whole flood of translations were coming.

The Bible had entered the modern age—the age of the individual.

12

THE BIBLE, IN OTHER WORDS

How would the early church fathers react if they walked into a modern church? Obviously, the world itself would provide plenty of culture shock for an ancient visitor—everything from automobiles and electricity to computers and cell phones. But they'd have to be particularly amazed by the forms the Bible has taken in the twenty-first century.

Thousands of years ago, papyrus was new technology, and it was revolutionary. So was parchment, and after that, the binding of pages into a book. Each of these innovations made the Bible accessible in a new way. The printing press brought mass production into the story. But after this, while technology continued to improve in the printing industry, the book remained the standard medium for scriptural presentation for hundreds of years. It was difficult to improve on bound, printed pages.

This was even true after the advent of radio. People still had their Bibles, but now it was also possible to hear preaching from a distance. In 1922, Paul Rader—a former cowboy, boxer, and football coach—became a preacher and one of the first to broadcast his church services. There was criticism; there always is when Christians embrace change. Radio was unbecoming of worship, and it might even kill the church!

But the Bible and the church survived and even thrived over the air. With television a few years later, the same developments occurred. Who could now imagine TV broadcasting without Bible-based programming?

Toward the end of the twentieth century, the introduction of the Internet represented an advance as profound as the printing press or the automobile. Ultimately it became possible for every church to broadcast, have an Internet presence, and take part in ministries and fellowship in ways no one could have imagined a generation ago.

If we accompanied one of the early church fathers on a time machine trip to the present—let's say Ignatius of Antioch—and brought him to church with us, he might notice some of the following:

The church library, near the front entrance, would have an amazing variety of Bibles. Many of these Bibles would be beautifully produced, a joy to hold, with eye-popping, colorful covers. Others would be leather or cowhide, cracked and faded by age and loving use. There would be colorful children's Bibles, translations in other languages, large-print editions, and an assortment of Bible-*related* volumes, such as Bible dictionaries, commentaries, atlases, and even fiction based on biblical characters. Ignatius would be startled to find some of his own writings in a reference work.

Then we'd visit an adult Sunday school class, and immediately Ignatius would notice that many of the participants were gazing at small devices—and we'd hastily explain that these provided full access to the Bible in multiple translations, daily devotionals with Scripture readings, and all the reference materials he had just seen in the library. Plus these little machines enable people to talk to someone far away!

Some would use tablets or even laptop computers for their Bible references. But everyone would go about these discussions as if there were nothing at all amazing about how they were getting the ancient Scriptures.

Suddenly there would be a voice, a bit "tinnier," coming out of a small speaker. And we'd see a camera. These would be connected to yet another computer. Two class members, we'd be told, are under the weather, and another is out of town, and all three are taking part in the class from a great distance, via technology! It's called teleconferencing.

Ignatius would whisper, "Just imagine if Paul had such a thing when he was in prison."

From there, we'd walk down the corridor to the church offices, for a quick visit with the pastor. He'd surely want to meet one of the early church fathers. We'd find him taking one last look at his sermon notes for the morning. Ignatius wouldn't be surprised, by this time, to see that a computer was involved. But the pastor would beckon Ignatius to come closer. "Let me show you what we can do," he'd say.

There on his screen we'd see the words from Romans 8—the morning text. The pastor would click his pointing device, and a window would open showing all kinds of information on that chapter—seven or eight biblical commentaries; a map of Paul's journeys; and a list of some of the important themes in Romans 8. Instead of walking to his bookshelf and pulling down heavy, dusty volumes to thumb through, his computer would open to the right references *for* him.

Then he'd point the cursor to a word in the Bible text: *justify*, in Romans 8:30. With one click, a screen would open up with a colorful table. He'd see the Greek version of the word, *dikaios*, and also a list of every other usage of the word in the New Testament.

Another click of the cursor would open a window showing ten different Bible translations of Romans 8:30. How long would it have taken to thumb through ten Bibles?

Technology has provided this generation with great power, speed, and availability of knowledge. The pastor only has to make use of it under God's guidance.

We'd excuse the pastor so he could attend to his pre-service prayer, then we'd find our seats in the church's lovely sanctuary. Ignatius would point with delight at one of the walls. "These windows with colored glass—they show our stories from the Scriptures! I like these best of all. Are these new inventions, too?"

"Not exactly," we'd say with a smile. "We've had those for a thousand years or so. Pretty low-tech. But watch the screen at the front."

Sure enough, a projection screen has lowered, and a high-definition film begins to play—nature scenes, with lovely music in surround sound, and, of course, Scripture verses in the forefront to prepare the congregation for worship. Simple, but so effective.

Later, the verses from Romans 8 would appear on the screen just as the pastor discussed each one. He'd make reference to the many people who are watching from home or listening to a podcast of the service. And he'd remind everyone that more materials on this subject will be available on the website during the week.

After the service, we're eager to hear which modern innovation most impressed Ignatius, our friend from the early years of Christianity. He'd think for a moment. "Well, I do love those windows, and how they dance in the sunlight," he says, "But my favorite, I think, was the pastor reciting the Scriptures so clearly and passionately. He stood before us and spoke the words of life. It's not much different from how it's done in my time, but it's the *best*. We feel the Lord's presence when His words are read before us, and God inhabits the praises of His people. I'm happy for those people who could join in from their screens, wherever they may be. It's amazing. All of these things are wonderful. But there's nothing like being here in the flesh when God fills the room, and there are no inventions as powerful as His Word."

Amen to that. Technology is one more tool for God to use. But it's merely another fashionable glove for His hand to fill. While the message remains the same, God's Word is as alive as ever, moving through the world in new and fascinating ways.

Perhaps most important of all, it's moving into corners of the world it has never entered across the centuries. The work of biblical translation is making that possible.

NEW LANGUAGES

Jesus's final command was to go into every nation, teaching and baptizing. (See Matthew 28:19.) In Acts 1:8, He says that His followers will be witnesses for Him in the farthest parts of the earth.

Yet after the first few generations of Christianity, there was no true missions movement until 1792, when William Carey founded the Baptist Missionary Society. Between then and now, Christianity had plenty of catching up to do, and missionaries have been sent to a great many nations where the gospel hadn't been heard.

Missionaries to China or Chile realized, of course, they would need the Bible in native languages. In many cases, missionaries spent years painstakingly learning languages and creating their own translations of the New Testament, and in time, perhaps the Old as well. During the nineteenth century, the Bible was translated into four hundred new languages.

But the task seemed to grow larger and larger, even as the world seemed to feel smaller with travel between nations becoming more common. In some communities, there were large and confounding numbers of dialects and local variations to consider.

William Cameron Townsend made that discovery as a missionary to Guatemala in 1917. He'd been a door-to-door Bible salesman in Southern California before deciding to become an international missionary. He arrived in a small coastal community called Santa Catarina and began to study the local Spanish dialect immediately because he'd quickly discovered his basic Spanish made no sense to many of the people he met. While he had a special interest in languages, he also poured himself into helping Guatemala's poor, founding a medical clinic, and filling other needs as he found them. But these people needed the Bible.

He respected the depth of work necessary to faithfully translate one language to another, and to that end founded the Summer Institute of Linguistics (SIL) to train translators. By 1942, SIL had grown considerably, and from it, Townsend created Wycliffe Bible Translators. By 1951, according to the organization, a complete Bible had been translated into one language; by the year 2000, there had been five hundred successful translations. Vision 2025 is an initiative to accelerate the process and at least see a translation effort in progress in all the remaining languages.

There are more than seven thousand languages in the world, by most estimates. Half the world's people speak one of twenty-three languages from that set, and obviously those languages have had the Bible for many years. But the others deserve one as well. More than one billion and a half people still don't have a full Bible, according to Wycliffe Global Alliance, as Townsend's original organization is now known. It's a gathering of organizations all cooperating with the intent of translating the Bible into every language.

But Wycliffe is one element in a growing movement. IllumiNations is another alliance of Bible translation agencies. Under its own umbrella, ten groups cooperate: American Bible Society, Biblica, Deaf Bible Society, Lutheran Bible Translators, Pioneer Bible Translators, Seed Company, SIL, The Word for the World, United Bible Societies, and Wycliffe USA.

We also must realize that not every language is spoken. In 2021, the Bible became available in American Sign Language (ASL) for the first time. The endeavor took forty years of work. The *American Sign Language Version* of the Bible is available, but there are more than four hundred sign languages to go.

On top of that, for the sight-impaired, the Bible is only translated into Braille in forty languages; a great many languages have no Braille code at all. This has been a sadly neglected area. Yes, audio Bibles can be produced, but the blind yearn to read the Bible for themselves just as those with sight do. Most people study by spending more time with one sentence (or verse) than an audio recording would offer. Braille Bibles would allow deeper studies and more fellowship with God.

So there's plenty of work to do, but technology and God's call to people are sending more harvesters into the field every day.

NEW UNDERSTANDINGS

Meanwhile, as the Bible moves outward to the world, there's an *inward* push to understand it even better. This has been an ongoing pursuit since the original authors received their inspiration and recorded it in words. What did Jesus mean by His parables? What are some of the subtle shades of Paul's terminology? How were the Psalms used in worship during the period when they were written?

The quest for understanding the Scriptures more clearly is never fulfilled; there are always new questions and new fields of investigation. Nineteenth-century scholars understood the Gospels in certain ways. They believed the four books were written later than the most recent evidence indicates. They interpreted the writings through methods that have since been questioned or even debunked. And in general, there's a far better understanding today of first-century Mediterranean culture, which is part of the milieu of the New Testament documents.

For example, there have been several *quests for the historical Jesus*, each one with a slightly different focus. In recent years, there have been attempts to better understand Jesus as a first-century Jewish rabbi, which means investigating other literature of the period to understand how parables were used, or why the Pharisees might have taken such exception to Jesus and His teachings.

Kenneth Bailey, author of *Jesus Through Middle Eastern Eyes*,[36] spent forty years living in the region of the Bible and helps readers to understand how people from that culture would have experienced Jesus. Richard Bauckham, on the other hand, offers a book called *Jesus and the Eyewitnesses*[37] that makes a strong, scholarly case for the Gospels as being the product of eyewitness testimony as opposed to strict oral tradition over generations.

The British theologian N. T. Wright has led what has been known as the "new perspective on Paul." He and other scholars maintain that since the Protestant Reformation, there's been a tendency to see Paul's Jewish mindset as overly legalistic in contrast to what Christ offered as salvation by grace. Their thinking is that the conditions of the Reformation—a reaction against the Catholic Church's abuses

36. Kenneth E. Bailey, *Jesus Through Middle Eastern Eyes: Cultural Studies in the Gospels* (Downers Grove, IL: InterVarsity Press, 2008).
37. Richard Bauckham, *Jesus and the Eyewitnesses: The Gospels as Eyewitness Testimony* (Grand Rapids, MI: Eerdmans Publishing Co., 2006).

of that time—and the particular Western way of seeing things have obscured what Paul actually wrote. The new perspective attempts to show that the idea of covenant with God was much more important to Hebrew theology of Paul's time than has been realized. This has proved to be an extremely controversial subject but has encouraged those on both sides to look at the Scriptures with fresh eyes.

Archaeology, too, continues to come up with fascinating discoveries. A few years ago, a stone tablet was unearthed in Caesarea that credited the edifice it supported to "Pontius Pilate, prefect of Judea." Before this, many critics had suggested Pilate was a figment of the gospel writers' imagination. Yet here was proof not only that Pilate existed, but that he was in authority during Jesus's lifetime, in accordance with the Gospels.

This is one example of many finds that have shed light on biblical topics, always seeming to confirm some contested name or place. The Gospel of John described in detail a pool with five porticos. For many years, the pool at Bethesda was assumed to be a fanciful invention of the author of John's gospel. Yet archaeologists eventually discovered the site—they just had to dig deeply enough.

When we do the same, there will always be something new to learn about the Bible.

NEW EDITIONS

Technology, as we've seen, has created new ways to experience the Bible; following the advent of radio came Hollywood films, then television, then audio recordings, then podcasts, and, of course, a wide range of Internet-based media. But the Bible itself has taken on a whole new wardrobe of outfits. The text itself can be presented in creative ways appropriate to whoever is reading it. This is happening in the form of new kinds of textual treatments.

The King James Version, with its occasional tweaks, dominated Bible reading for nearly 350 years. This isn't to say there weren't occasional attempts at dressing up the Bible in new fashions. A version called "an American Translation" was released in 1935 by translators Smith and Goodspeed, but it's now difficult to find a copy. Far more impactful was the *Revised Standard Version*, with the full Bible arriving in 1952. The *Jerusalem Bible* of 1966 was a successful Catholic Bible that was widely admired for its lovely prose.

But little could compare to the success of Ken Taylor's *Living Bible*, first appearing in 1971. As a paraphrase rather than a translation, it veered sharply from the familiar text—particularly the King James text—and was well-timed for a baby-boom generation that was just then coming of age in Sunday school classes and youth groups and primed for a Bible that spoke in a casual manner. Dr. Taylor paraphrased his version on train rides during his commute, with the intention of having a Bible suitable for his children. Millions of children and even more adults benefited.

Positioned almost as a counterpunch was the *New American Standard Bible*, also 1971, which was a staunchly literal translation. What it lost in contemporary, casual lingo, it more than gained in precise, word-for-word translation of the original.

Today's *English Version*, known later as the *Good News Bible*, appeared in a full Bible version in 1976, but it had stolen a march on the *Living Bible* in New Testament form as *Good News for Modern Man* in 1966. While technically a translation, it had the feel of a paraphrase and also contained stylish line drawings.

With the blockbuster success of the *New International Version*, released in full in 1984, the flood began to intensify. The NIV quickly became the favorite Bible of evangelical churches, replacing for many readers the perceived dryness of the *New American Standard* and the seeming flippancy of the *Living Bible*. The NIV struck a middle course, though no Bible version is without its detractors. In time, the NIV, too, was found wanting by some critics.

The *English Standard Version* of 2001 became another favorite in evangelical churches. Based on the *Revised Standard Version*, it strove as much as possible for a literal translation while attempting to solve the problems of difficult translation issues in the ancient text. The ESV was particularly notable for its combination with one of the most thorough study Bible editions yet, and it made use of online access to improve on some of the features.

The following year, Eugene Peterson's personal translation, *The Message*, was released. Peterson's gift was a wonderful fluency with the English language and an ability to recreate the passion found, say, in the Psalms or in the writings of Paul. While many passages seemed at first glance to wander far afield from the original, they always demonstrated a deep understanding of the actual meaning of those passages. Peterson's special target audience was people who would ordinarily never pick up a Bible and who would be confounded by *churchy language*.

Meanwhile, the King James Version showed no signs of going out of print. In monthly bestseller lists, it usually came in second to the *New International Version*, dropping in recent times to fourth place.[38] But there was also the *New King James Version*, a refinement of the KJV, and also the *King James Version Easy Read Bible* (KJVER), which replaced the archaic thees and thous but remained faithful to the text. If the NIV had built an impressive following in a generation or so, how many generations could the KJV boast as a beloved Bible?

By the twenty-first century, all of these translations and many more were available on the Internet and in frequent use through that medium. As a matter of fact, readers could now examine different translations for comparison and contrast thanks to popular Bible applications on cell phones and other electronic media.

This also began to raise questions: Why are all these translations so different? Why does *The Message* read one way and the *English Standard Version* another?

It's important to understand how biblical versions work.

---

38. "Bible Translations Bestsellers, January 2023," from the Evangelical Christian Publishers Association, accessed May 19, 2023, christianbookexpo.com/bestseller/translations.php?id=0123.

NEW APPROACHES

For many years, there was one approach to biblical translation: word-for-word conversion, one language to another. It's a simple idea. What does this Hebrew or Greek word mean, and what word in our present language means the same thing?

Over time, at least two major problems with this strategy came to light. The first is rather obvious. The time and culture lapse between ancient Israel and any modern nation presents a huge obstacle. While the spiritual problems of humanity never really change, the daily details of humanity and everyday culture vary enormously. It's no simple matter to understand the complex world of, say, first century Judea, a region with Jewish traditions, Greek language and culture seeping in, and Roman rule. But also, when sums of money are discussed, what are their values? What does a Roman procurator do? What is a Syro-Phoenician woman? A Zealot? A Sadducee? And why were tax collectors so despised?

Certainly we could all go back to school and study biblical culture, but few Bible study or Sunday school attendees are likely to do that. Our Bibles need to give us some help, and simply having the closest words in our language still leaves us wondering too often.

The other problem is a bit more subtle. In attempting to convert one word to another, language to language, any scholar will tell you that the languages don't cooperate. Every language works differently, and there actually may be *no* English word to match a given Hebrew word. Or the best match may really be a mismatch.

A famous example of this is *agape*, the Greek word Paul uses for love in his famous first letter to the early church at Corinth. (See 1 Corinthians 13.) *Love* is certainly the best word choice in English, but it doesn't tell the whole story. The Greeks have other words that we'd also translate as love. One, *philia*, denotes a brotherly love; another, *eros*, means an erotic love. A third, *storge*, is the natural affection a parent feels for a child. Paul chooses a word that means an unconditional, sacrificial love—the love perfected only in God.

A translator comes to *agape* and wonders what can be done to get this highly specific meaning across. After all, *agape* is the essence of Christian behavior. There are certainly limits to what a strict, word-to-word translation can accomplish.

CATEGORIES OF TRANSLATIONS

There's also what we might call a marketing angle. Those who sell Bibles want a product that satisfies the largest audience and offers a positive, inspiring experience in Bible study. We have a great number of Bible translations to choose from. This is partly a quest to find the niche that serves a particular audience while also selling as many Bibles as possible. What kinds of Bibles will do that? There are three general categories of translations.

FORMAL EQUIVALENCE

This is the simplest and most traditional approach to Bible translation. It's known informally as literal translation; the attempt is to simply analyze the Hebrew and Greek manuscripts as effectively and accurately as possible, then transmit the meanings, word for word, into the modern language. As much as possible, this strategy pays attention even to the grammatical structure of the original material.

For example, the apostle Paul rarely used short sentences. The first chapter of Ephesians is filled with extremely lengthy ones, including a sentence that moves through ten verses and is 212 words long. (See Ephesians 1:3–14.) We tend to come up for air when we can find a comma, but there's also a vast library of theological ideas tucked away in that sequence. A literal translation is overwhelming.

In the past, the formal equivalence approach has respected Paul's grammatical structure as being part and parcel of God's revelation. This can be difficult for the reader at times, but serious Bible students often desire to be as close as possible to the words that were written two thousand years ago. If that takes a bit more concentration, so be it. And after a while, one becomes accustomed to the odd Greek sentence structure. In general, formal equivalence translations are more accurate, but more difficult to read.

Popular examples of formal equivalence Bibles include:

+ The King James Version
+ The *New American Standard Bible*
+ The *New King James Version*
+ The *Revised Standard* and *New Revised Standard* versions
+ The *English Standard Version*

DYNAMIC EQUIVALENCE

This more modern approach, created by linguist E. A. Nida, attempts to take into consideration the obstacles of language translation by considering not just the text, but also the audience and what they will likely understand. Instead of a word-for-word correspondence, dynamic equivalence seeks a thought-for-thought equivalence.

Philippians 2:6 has the literal translation concerning Jesus as *"who, being in the form of God."* What does *"the form of God"* mean? The *New International Version* (NIV), a dynamic equivalence translation, renders this as, *"Who, being in very nature God."* Many scholars would say this communicates Paul's meaning effectively.

But it also opens the door to controversy. Interpretation is now allowed, even required; there's an opening for the kind of nuance that might pull a verse in one theological direction or the other. Therefore some Bible readers distrust dynamic equivalence translations. Others, however, are deeply grateful to read sentences structured in the style of modern conversation. They have no problem with an editor dividing Paul's marathon greeting of the Ephesians into manageable sentences, and they'll trust the translation committee to make the judgment calls that help to make a verse like Philippians 2:6 comprehensible. What matters most is our understanding the Scriptures and receiving inspiration from them as effectively as possible.

In general, dynamic equivalence translations are less accurate, but easier to understand.

Popular examples of dynamic equivalence Bibles include:

+ The *New International Version*
+ The *Good News Bible*
+ The *Contemporary English Version*
+ The *New Living Translation*

FREE (PARAPHRASE)

There will always be readers attracted to the simplest and perhaps most vibrant expression of the Scriptures. Strictly speaking, a paraphrase is not a translation at all but a full rewriting of the scriptural passage with a view toward remaining true to its heart without being burdened by difficult language. New or younger Christians find this form of Bible ideal. Clearly it's the easiest style to understand, although it's also the least accurate. Sometimes biblical metaphors or objects—such as farming tools or ancient clothing, for example—are completely thrown out in favor of using more contemporary words to make the point. For those who know the Bible very well, it can be a little unsettling to hear a passage utterly transformed beyond recognizability. But paraphrase approaches are very helpful for some readers, and they also have the advantage of capturing the freshness and passion that the original manuscripts must have had. Eugene Peterson, the late author of *The Message*, often does this. Advanced readers are less likely to use his work as a primary Bible, but will keep it on hand as a kind of commentary or a resource to help others understand the passage.

Popular examples of this type include:

+ The *Living Bible*
+ The *Message*

This short tour of translation styles makes the situation appear more clearcut than it really is. Most translations have at least some flexibility. Dynamic equivalence Bibles will go for literal expression whenever possible, while trying to strike a balance. Formal equivalence Bibles compromise occasionally for the sake of salvaging meaning for the reader.

A well-known example is 1 Peter 1:13; the King James Version reads, *"Wherefore gird up the loins of your mind, be sober"* (KJV). That first part is an interesting turn of phrase that would literally mean, "Pull up the pants of your brain." Newer readers, of course, won't recognize the common biblical phrase, "Gird up your loins" at all. What should the translator do?

The *Revised Standard Version* of 1952, still listed as a formal equivalence translation, gives this as, *"Therefore gird up your minds"* (1 Peter 1:13 RSV), a compromise that got the idea across while still using the aging verb, *gird*. Even so, the metaphor doesn't really work.

The *New International Version* demonstrated its dynamic equivalence approach by using, *"With minds that are alert and fully sober"* (NIV). This is the meaning of the passage, but we lose the wonderful word picture of hitching up one's mantle or cloak to make a run for it. Most translations since then have followed suit with similar phrases.

But *The Message* came up with this presentation: *"So roll up your sleeves, get your head in the game, be totally ready"* (1 Peter 1:13 MSG). It takes a genuine dexterity with words to capture "gird up your loins" in the modern phrase "roll up your sleeves." This retains the clothing metaphor and manages to capture the meaning in a vivid way.

The parade of new Bible editions will continue, but no matter how we dress it up, the Word of God is still ageless and timeless.

A NEW DAY

A few decades ago, Alvin Toffler wrote his classic study *Future Shock*.[39] He looked back on the trajectory of change in the twentieth century and predicted that technology would continue to evolve

---

39. Alvin Toffler, *Future Shock* (New York: Bantam Books, 1970).

at an ever-rapid pace as the twenty-first century approached, until humanity reeled with dizziness, unable to continue adjusting to the accelerating transition.

This has been the case, particularly in the era of the microchip. The Internet has changed daily life profoundly. And with all the gains science has made—in the fields of medicine, transportation, commerce, communication, and even space travel—the basic problems of humanity remain. Life may be better than in our grandparents' time in incremental ways, particularly in terms of convenience, but there's a sense that certain values have been lost too. Science couldn't prevent a deadly virus that swept across the world. It isn't preventing new wars from starting up, nor is the crime rate dropping. As for "peace on earth," the greatest conflicts are often within nations rather than outside them.

We have massive numbers of friends on social media, yet we feel lonely and disconnected. Technology has put tremendous power in our hands, yet we feel small and weak. We wonder sometimes whether this human race is approaching the finish line.

As we confront these discouraging feelings, we turn to the one thing that doesn't change: the Word of God. We can experience His presence in more ways than ever before through fresh technology, but the truth is still the truth. God still speaks through these pages, whether on stone, papyrus, parchment, vellum, paper, or screen. And no matter how dark the world grows, the Light of the World drives out that darkness.

We can't know what the future holds for the Bible, but we do know what the Bible holds for the future—hope, wisdom, joy, peace, and guidance.

Can we make the best use of those intangible, immortal gifts? Can we find new ways to share them? The answer must be *yes* because behind these amazing Scriptures is a living God, and with Him, *"all things are possible"* (Matthew 19:26).

BIBLIOGRAPHY

Archer, Gleason, Jr. *A Survey of Old Testament Introduction*. 3rd. ed. Chicago: Moody Press, 1994.

Barton, John. *A History of the Bible: The Book and Its Faiths*. New York: Viking, 2019.

Brannan, Rick, trans. *The Apostolic Fathers in English*. Bellingham, WA: Lexham Press, 2012.

Brannan, Rick. "Apostolic Fathers." In *The Lexham Bible Dictionary*, edited by John D. Barry, et al. Bellingham, WA: Lexham Press, 2016.

Bruce, F. F. *The Canon of Scripture*. Downers Grove, IL: InterVarsity Press, 1988.

Douglas, J. D., Philip Wesley Comfort, and Donald Mitchell. *Who's Who in Christian History*. Wheaton, IL: Tyndale House, 1992.

Galli, Mark, and Ted Olsen. *131 Christians Everyone Should Know*. Nashville, TN: Broadman & Holman Publishers, 2000.

Gamble, Harry Y. *The New Testament Canon: Its Making and Meaning*. Eugene, OR: Wipf & Stock, 2002.

Geisler, Norman L., and William E. Nix. *A General Introduction to the Bible*. Rev. and expanded. Chicago: Moody Press, 1986.

Green, Joel B., Scot McKnight, and I. Howard Marshall, eds. *Dictionary of Jesus and the Gospels*. Downers Grove, IL: InterVarsity Press, 1992.

Guthrie, Donald. *New Testament Introduction*. 4th rev. ed. The Master Reference Collection. Downers Grove, IL: InterVarsity Press, 1996.

Herklots, H. G. G. *How Our Bible Came to Us.* Oxford: Oxford University Press, 1954.

Kloha, Jeffrey. "The Day the Bible Became a Bestseller." Text and Canon. September 21, 2022. textandcanon.org/the-day-the-bible-became-a-bestseller.

Lightfoot, Neil R. *How We Got the Bible.* Grand Rapids: Baker Books, 2003.

Marshall, I. Howard. *New Testament Theology: Many Witnesses, One Gospel.* Downers Grove, IL: InterVarsity Press, 2004.

Metzger, Bruce M. *The Canon of the New Testament: Its Origin, Development, and Significance.* New York: Oxford University Press, 1987.

McDonald, Lee Martin, and James A. Sanders, eds. *The Canon Debate.* Grand Rapids: Baker Academic, 2001.

Nida, E. A., and C. R. Taber. *The theory and practice of translation.* Boston: Brill, 2003.

Osborne, Margaret. "Scientists Translate the Oldest Sentence Written in the First Alphabet." Smithsonian, November 10, 2022. https://bit.ly/3knd4Tk.

Rutledge, Howard and Phyllis Rutledge. *In the Presence of Mine Enemies: Seven years a POW in North Vietnam.* Grand Rapids: Fleming Revell, 1973.

Scholer, David M. "How We Got Our Bible." *Christian History* 43 (1994).

Spivey, Mark, "Historic Family Bible Crown Jewels of N. J. Library." *USA Today,* January 18, 2013.

Warfield, Benjamin B. *The Canon of the New Testament: How and When Formed.* Philadelphia: American Sunday-School Union, 1892.

Weigle, Luther A. "English Versions Since 1611." In *The Cambridge History of the Bible: The West from the Reformation to the Present Day*, edited by S. I. Greenslade. London: Cambridge, 2008.

APPENDIX A:
SELECTIVE TIMELINE OF
BIBLICAL HISTORY

c. 1400–400 BC	Hebrew Old Testament written
c. 250–200 BC	The Septuagint, a Greek translation of the Old Testament, is created
AD 45–90?	Greek New Testament written
140–150	Marcion creates his own, severely edited New Testament
303–306	Diocletian destroys many New Testament Scriptures during persecution
305–310	Lucian of Antioch's Greek New Testament text completed; becomes a foundation for later Bibles
367	Athanasius's Festal Letter lists complete New Testament canon (27 books) for the first time
397	Council of Carthage establishes Orthodox New Testament canon (27 books)
400	Jerome translates the Bible into Latin; his Vulgate becomes the standard of medieval church
650	Caedmon, a monk, sets Bible books to verse
1380–1382	John Wycliffe and associates translate full Bible into English

1388	John Purvey creates a revision of the Wycliffe Bible.
1455	Gutenberg's Latin Bible is the first printed book
1516	Erasmus's Greek New Testament is used by KJV translators
1525	William Tyndale makes the first translation of the New Testament from Greek into English
1536	Tyndale strangled and burned
1537	Miles Coverdale's Bible completes Tyndale's work on the Old Testament
1538	Great Bible, assembled by John Rogers, is the first English Bible authorized for public use
1560	Geneva Bible—the work of William Whittingham, a Protestant English exile in Geneva—is published
1568	Bishops' Bible revises the Great Bible
1582	Douay-Rheims New Testament published
1611	King James Version, the "Authorized Version," is published
1762	Correction of spelling and punctuation in the King James Version by Dr. F. S. Paris
1780	Robert Raikes begins Sunday school movement, teaching the Bible to needy children
1782	Robert Aitken produces first English language Bible printed in America (King James)
1791	Isaac Collins prints the first family Bible and first illustrated Bible printed in America (King James)

1819	Thomas Jefferson creates so-called Jefferson Bible, a life of Jesus that omits miraculous passages
1822	Earliest Chinese version of the Bible
1846	Illuminated Bible, printed in USA, with large number of illustrations
1863	Young's Literal Translation
1876	Full Bible published for use in Russian Orthodox Church
1899	Gideons International founded
1901	*American Standard Version*: first major American King James Revision
1906	Albert Schweitzer publishes *Quest of the Historical Jesus*
1922	Moffatt translation published by James Moffatt
1924	First religious radio station, KFUO AM
1942	Founding of Wycliffe Bible Translators
1945	Nag Hammadi library of ancient texts discovered
1947	Dead Sea Scrolls discovered
1952	*Revised Standard Version*
1956	Anchor Bible Commentary series begins
1963	US Supreme Court prohibits reading of Bible in public schools
1965	Second Vatican Council allows the Mass in vernacular language
1970	Beginning of "Jesus movement" in the United States
1971	*New American Standard Bible*

1971   *The Living Bible*

1975   Scholar Bruce Metzger publishes *Textual Commentary on the Greek New Testament*

1977   E. P. Sanders begins "new perspective on Paul" movement

1978   *New International Version*

1978   Chicago Statement on Biblical Inerrancy

1979   *The Jesus Film* is produced by Campus Crusade for Christ; later it becomes the most viewed film in the world

1982   *New King James Version*

1985   Jesus Seminar, an association of liberal gospel scholars, founded by Robert Funk

2002   *English Standard Version*

2004   *Holman Christian Standard Version* (HCSV)

2006   *New English Translation*, offering verse-by-verse textual detail

2014   *Modern English Version*

2017   *Christian Standard Bible* (full revision of HCSV)

2023   *King James Version Easy Read Bible* updated

APPENDIX B:
THE AMAZING STORY OF
CODEX SINAITICUS

There are four great *uncial codices* in the world—full Bible texts in Greek. The oldest of these is the Codex Sinaiticus, which is often called the Sinai Bible because it was found at the foot of Mount Sinai, one of the greatest of biblical sites.

This is the traditional site where Moses received the law, including the Ten Commandments, from God. It's also the site of one of the oldest monasteries, Saint Catherine's, which was built in the sixth century. It stands in the place where monks claimed another great event happened: Moses hearing from God in the form of a burning bush.

In 1844, Constantin von Tischendorf, then age twenty-nine, decided to pay a visit there, having heard about a library with a collection of very old manuscripts. He was an almost obsessive student of the New Testament texts, and it was his mission to find manuscripts that hadn't yet been located. At that date, in the middle of the nineteenth century, quite a few still remained to be found.

Tischendorf believed that somewhere there were enough undiscovered scraps of parchment that, if assembled together, would reveal precisely what the original authors of the New Testament wrote. He'd already published a critical edition of the Greek New Testament, based on the limits of what was then known.

While still a young man, Tischendorf enjoyed some significant scholarly triumphs and raised the funds to visit museums and libraries across Europe, always enlarging his knowledge. Then he decided to dig deeper by searching in the Middle East itself. When he arrived at Saint Catherine's Monastery at Sinai, he found lodgings nearby and gained entrance to the monastery library. It was sadly neglected, filled with deterioration and decay. Tischendorf had harbored great hopes for this site, but as he looked at the volumes and holdings, those hopes began to dissipate. In the mid-nineteenth century, travel was expensive, difficult, and time-consuming. He had ridden camels to get there. Disappointment was debilitating.

But then, as he turned from the shelves, his eye fell on a basket filled with piles of old papers, seemingly discarded as waste. He asked the librarian about these and was told that this was the third basket of scraps headed for the flames due to their deteriorated condition. The first two had already been burned.

Glancing through the basket, Tischendorf was shocked to recognize biblical phrases written in Greek. And yes, the pages had seen better days, but these appeared to be some of the oldest scriptural manuscripts he'd ever seen. The pages were fine vellum, and the handwriting was strong and sure.

With perhaps too much eagerness in his eyes, Tischendorf managed to gain permission to take some of this "scrap" with him. A third of the basket was the agreement. Most monasteries by this time had heard about *manuscript raiders* searching for ancient treasure, and often willing to walk away with what didn't belong to them. The monks at St. Catherine's may not have been taking good care of their library, but they were cautious about giving up its contents.

Tischendorf did some copying; he was finding passages from Isaiah and Jeremiah. The monks assured him that they wouldn't do any more burning and would give better care to what was in the basket. Traveling home, Tischendorf excitedly published his findings without revealing their source.

For various reasons, including a busy agenda of scholarship in other directions, it was nine years before he could return to Sinai. But he was in for a bitter disappointment. No one in the entire monastery recognized him or knew what he was talking about. The basket, of course, was gone without a trace. Yet somehow, as he scoured every inch of the library, he came across a bookmark made from a document whose handwriting he recognized. It was the same Greek he knew so well, from the 1844 finding. A bookmark! And this time the reference was Genesis 24, telling him there was even more of the Septuagint yet to find. If the prophets and Genesis were part of one manuscript, this implied the full Old Testament was there at the very least.

Maybe this small bookmark was all that was left. Tischendorf hoped with all his heart it wasn't true, but sure enough, he found nothing more. And eventually, he gave up his secret as to where he'd made his earlier discovery. He suggested that once a full Old Testament had been there, maybe a full Bible—but that someone else had carried away what he hadn't secured. At this point, with seemingly nothing more to find, he at least wanted credit for being the first to discover fragments at Mount Sinai.

A SURPRISE DISCOVERY

In 1859, Alexander II, czar of Russia, funded one more visit to Sinai for Tischendorf. After all this time, it must have seemed like a last, desperate attempt. Once again, he found a room and checked into the neglected, all-but-abandoned library. Unsurprisingly there were no more Septuagint traces. He did thumb through some of the other holdings of the library, then told his hosts to gather the camels and make preparations for the return trip.

Tischendorf took one more early evening walk with a steward who invited him to his small room for refreshment. At that point, the steward suddenly told him he, too, had been reading pieces of a

Septuagint. And he produced a large parcel, all wrapped in red cloth, and displayed what was inside.

Tischendorf couldn't believe his eyes. He immediately recognized the old, familiar fragments, but also most of the rest of the Old Testament, as well as a complete New Testament, a portion of the Shepherd of Hermas, and the Epistle of Barnabas. Mustering all of his composure, Tischendorf expressed interest without giving full vent to his exhilaration. As casually as possible, he asked, "Would you have any objection to my taking these manuscripts to my room, where I can examine them more closely?" The steward was happy to acquiesce.

He was holding what he believed to be the world's oldest Bible, an incredibly valuable assemblage of information from the ancient world about the greatest body of writing in human history. All that he'd discovered in the past—including some impressive pieces—paled before what was now in his hands. His original goal was to put together an ancient New Testament piece by piece, all of different manuscripts. That was the best that could be expected then. But here was a full New Testament, complete in itself.

Tischendorf wasn't about to sleep that night, not with what sat beside his bed. Instead he stayed awake and made a hand copy of Barnabas, the reason being that it was a *lost book* that hadn't turned up until now. The Epistle of Barnabas had once been on the fringe of acceptance in the canon, at least to some, but no one had a complete version.

The next morning, he began discussions about the future of the document and his more immediate task of making hand copies. Tischendorf offered nearly everything in his power to give for outright possession, but neither the monastery nor the steward would accept. So he made it known that for something as extensive as copying a full Bible, he'd need to work from Cairo. This was another sore topic, but Tischendorf managed to find the right man for that decision and get him to sign off on it.

Two weeks later, Tischendorf, two assistants, and the manuscript were in Cairo, with the three men working patiently, straining their eyes; many corrections had been scrawled over the original writing. There were notes and alterations. It was tedious work, but in two months, the job was done—at least for a bare sketch of what had been found. There are many nuances in the study of the handwriting (paleography) that cried out for intensive study. Later, further work would establish that the Sinai Bible was the product of three different scribes, each with their own style and idiosyncrasies.

Tischendorf was pleased, but he still wanted a truly accurate edition of the manuscript. He suggested to the monks that they make the manuscript a gift to the Russian czar. After some time, there was an agreement on this strategy, although what was agreed upon, and whether Tischendorf acted honorably, are matters still debated. Meanwhile, Tischendorf decided to use printing presses to publish an exact reproduction. Today, this wouldn't be a complex task, but at that time, it was a huge project because of the different colors of inks, missing letters, and other tiny but significant details. Everything was minutely hand-copied, and the results were printed as three hundred full-size copies, all presented to the czar, who sent most of them to thrilled scholars and libraries in various places.

All of these developments were great days for scholarship, but there was still the question of the original manuscript. Now that its value was established, it couldn't be left to the elements in a drafty monastery. The monks were very hesitant to make any permanent agreement but did agree to a temporary loan. In 1869, twenty-five years after Tischendorf's first visit to Sinai, ownership passed to the czar, with a generous financial reward given to the monastery.

In 1933, the Russian government sold the Codex Sinaiticus to the British Library, where it can now be studied closely by scholars. It arrived in London by train with great ceremony, and it's said that when the manuscript package was removed from the car, all of the men took off their hats in a show of respect.

Current scholarship agrees that the manuscript was copied in the middle of the fourth century—that is, a few years after the Council of Nicaea and around the time Constantine commissioned Eusebius to produced fifty copies of the Bible. Could this be one of them? It's doubtful, though it does bear much in common with the second-oldest Bible, which is kept in the Vatican. The Sinai Bible attests to a canon established quite early and in similar order to modern Bibles. While The Shepherd and Barnabas are included, they're placed at the end, clearly showing their inferior status.

While this is the oldest and *most* complete Bible in the world, it has never been *fully* complete, always been missing a few leaves, all from the Old Testament. It also helps us establish certain additions to the verses as being absent in earlier versions—the disputed ending to Mark's Gospel, for example.

But in 1975, there was a new twist to an already fascinating story. A fire broke out at Saint Catherine's, and new discoveries were made during the cleanup. A ceiling collapse two centuries earlier had cut off access to an old room and buried quite a trove of manuscripts. But now, at least twelve new pages to the Sinai Bible were recovered, as well as an impressive number of unrelated but very old documents, including sixty-seven Greek New Testaments.

Codex Sinaiticus, along with the other most ancient uncials, gives us a clear glimpse of what the Bible looked like near the dawn of Christianity.

ABOUT THE AUTHOR

A versatile and creative author, editor, and storyteller, Rob Suggs has written or collaborated on more than sixty books. His clients have included *New York Times* best-selling authors such as Kyle Idleman, Lee Strobel, Mark Batterson, David Jeremiah, and Bruce Wilkinson.

Rob worked with Jeremy and Jennifer Williams on *Tenacious: How God Used a Terminal Diagnosis to Turn a Family and a Football Team into Champions*, which is being turned into a movie. Rob also co-authored several books with family counselor Dr. Ross Campbell, including *How to Really Love Your Angry Child*. Among Rob's solo efforts are *The Comic Book Bible*, *Christmas Ate My Family*, and *Top Dawg: Mark Richt and the Revival of Georgia Football*.

A graduate of Furman University, Rob served for three years as a senior editor at Walk Through the Bible Ministries. An experienced teacher and preacher, Rob has led a four-part seminar on how the Bible came to be. He wrote and illustrated a six-part history of Christianity for *His* magazine published by InterVarsity Press. He also wrote the LifeGuide Bible studies *The Ten Commandments* and *Christian Community*.

For two decades, Rob contributed many cartoons to *Christianity Today* and *Leadership Journal*. Collections of these cartoons were published in the books *It Came from Beneath the Pew* and *Preacher from the Black Lagoon*.

Rob is a fourth-generation native of Atlanta, Georgia. He and his wife Gayle have two adult children. Readers may connect with Rob at www.robsuggs.com.